Party and Holiday Decorations You Can Make

by Karen Carlson McCann

with Sue T. Garmon

Drawings and Photographs
by Karen Carlson McCann

AVENEL BOOKS • NEW YORK

To

Stephen and Kirsten

Frances and Walter

with love

K.C.McC.

0-517-129612

Copyright © MCMLXX by Karen Carlson McCann
All rights reserved.

Library of Congress Catalog Card Number: 70-111177

This edition is published by Avenel Books
a division of Crown Publishers, Inc.
by arrangement with Doubleday & Company

b c d e f g h

Manufactured in the United States Of America

Preface

While creating and compiling projects for CREATIVE HOME DECORATIONS YOU CAN MAKE, a number of interested friends (including the editors) expressed their hope that the book would contain, in addition to suggestions for decorating and beautifying the home, some ideas for party and holiday decorations.

Since my original intention was to present a smörgåsbord of ideas—something to appeal to every reader—a number of such projects was included in the original manuscript and was intended for publication in that book.

However, that section of the manuscript dealing with party and holiday decorations continued to grow. It soon became apparent that it would not be possible to include it all unless the book were to reach monumental proportions. Therefore, at the request of the editors, that section was omitted from CREATIVE HOME DECORATIONS YOU CAN MAKE. It has been expanded to produce this second volume.

Parties and holidays offer endless opportunities for decoration. Time and space would not permit a book containing all of the various possibilities, but we have tried to include a variety of party and holiday themes.

If you've read CREATIVE HOME DECORATIONS YOU CAN MAKE and have tried a few of the projects, you'll know that decorating is fun. You'll also have learned that these projects are inexpensive to make; but more important, they're distinctive, different—and uniquely your own!

Introduction

Decorator accessories are definitely "in," and if you've priced them at various boutique shops, you'll have found that they can be quite expensive. It's much more fun to make your own—and it's much easier on your budget!

Whether you know it or not, you DO have a flair for decorating. Everyone does! A few of you may need a bit more encouragement and advice than others to discover and cultivate this flair.

The ideas in this book should give any latent creative instincts a nudge and are designed to stimulate them to their fullest development. The projects are especially geared to require relatively little time, money or equipment. They will, in addition to furnishing you with imaginative decorator accessories, provide you with many hours of pleasurable diversion from your daily routine.

Every party, holiday and season of the year offers you an opportunity to express yourself creatively. You'll discover the tremendous satisfaction that comes from creating something yourself, and at the same time you'll find an outlet for those creative instincts and urges which are born in all of us. But more than that, this is a form of recreation; it's an emotional catharsis, a form of escape, a method of therapy. In short, it's just plain good medicine to work with your hands!

The simplest party or the most elaborate social event gives you a chance to show off your decorative talents. You don't have to be an art expert—let your imagination run riot, have fun, and go ahead and try!

Contents

Contents

Party Decorations

A party is a mood, a time, a place, a person, a happening. A party is warmth, laughter, small talk and fun. It's a light heart, a quick smile and lots of love.

And because a party is such a special thing, the decorations which you use for it should be something special, too.

Party decorations which are bought in stores have a typical synthetic gaiety, are quite expensive and are depressingly similar to those used by everyone else. But your party decor can and should reflect your own individual taste, style and personality.

People make parties, and people are different. So let your decorations express *your* difference!

FESTIVE TABLECLOTHS

Colorful tablecloths of your own creation, designed to complement your decorative schemes, will provide the crowning touch of originality to your party decor and enhance that look of expansive hospitality which says, "Welcome to our house! We're glad you came!"

Fabric Tablecloth

Cotton and blends come in a wide variety of colors, are relatively inexpensive and launder like a dream. A bit of one of these fabrics picked up at a remnant sale can be whipped into a pretty and practical tablecloth in a matter of minutes.

Choose a vivid or subtle shade, solid color or lively print to accent your centerpiece and decorations.

MATERIALS NEEDED:

fabric—choose cotton or a washable blend

thread—to accent or match the color of the fabric

needle or sewing machine
tape measure
scissors
fringe or braid (*optional*)—to match or contrast with the fabric and long enough to trim the edges on all four sides of the tablecloth.

DIRECTIONS:

Measure the length and width of the top of your table, and then add 24 inches to both the width and the length. This will tell you how much fabric will be needed to make your tablecloth.

Plan your table decorations before selecting your fabric. By proceeding in this manner you will be able to complement your decor with a cloth of an appropriate color.

When you buy the material, be sure to consult the dimensions of your table. If your table is very broad, you may have to do a little figuring and allow for a seam down the middle to make the tablecloth wide enough.

Cut the material to the desired dimensions, sewing a seam down the middle if necessary.

Make the hem about ¼ inch, turning the material under twice to hide the raw edges. This may be sewed on the machine or by hand, using small stitches.

For a really fancy party look, braid or fringe may be sewed around the edges of the tablecloth.

Net Tablecloth

White or colored net used over a white or colored cloth or sheet gives a really elegant look to your table.

Mix or match colors, make it as simple or elaborate as you please to provide a striking background for your decor.

Net gives the appearance of luxury, but it's actually quite inexpensive, so you can have a new cloth for every special occasion.

MATERIALS NEEDED:

nylon net—a color of your choice
tape measure
scissors
tablecloth—this is used under the net cloth, so choose a color which will look attractive with the colored net. Use a fabric tablecloth you've made, a colored or white sheet or a ready-made cloth.
braid or fringe (*optional*)—gold, silver, or a color to match or complement the net
felt (*optional*)—a matching or accent color
sequins (*optional*)—a matching or accent color
beads (optional)—a matching or accent color

DIRECTIONS:

First, select a colored or white tablecloth to be used under the net. Then decide what color net you would like to use over this, keeping in mind the table decorations you have planned to use.

For example, you might spark your table with the Christmas colors by using green or red net over a white cloth. White net used over a white cloth is both formal and feminine, and is ideal for a bridal party. A yellow tablecloth topped with pale green net is cool and springlike and is suitable for almost any occasion, and an orange cloth covered with black net is perfect for Halloween. The possibilities are endless.

Once you have selected a tablecloth, measure it to determine its length and width. You will want to buy enough net to make the finished net tablecloth the same size as the fabric cloth under it. If you have an extremely wide table it may be necessary to sew two widths of net together.

When you have selected your net, cut it to the correct dimensions, making a seam down the middle if necessary. Net will not ravel, so you do not have to allow for a hem.

This net covering may be used as it is, or you can add interest and excitement by trimming the net with decorations selected to reflect varying holiday and party themes. Fancy braid, fringe, felt cutouts, beads or sequins may be sewed or glued to the net, and arranged in formal patterns or scattered in a carefully haphazard fashion over the cloth.

The quickest way to embellish your net cloth is to sew a row or two of braid around the edges. Braids are now made in an extremely wide array of lovely styles and luscious colors, and you're sure to find several that will set your cloth off to perfection.

Card Table Cover

Scalloped edges and braid trimmings give this attractive felt cloth a real party look.

It's just the thing to dress up a plain card table or disguise a somewhat battered one for those "friendly little games."

MATERIALS NEEDED:

felt—a 45-inch square in a color of your choice
scissors
pencil
saucer or small plate
thread—the same color as the braid
braid—about 7 yards, a color to complement the felt
needle
pins

DIRECTIONS:

To scallop the edges of the felt square, start by laying the felt flat on the floor or on a large table.

Select a small plate or saucer to use as a pattern for making the scallops even.

Begin by placing the plate in the center of one side of the felt square. The plate's edge should be barely touching the edge of the felt. Then, with a pencil, trace around the bottom half of the plate to make one scallop.

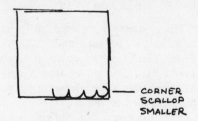

CORNER
SCALLOP
SMALLER

When you have finished drawing scallops on all four sides, cut along your pencil lines. (Incidentally, felt doesn't ravel, so there is no need to hem it.)

Finally, pin and sew braid to the edges of all the scallops. You may have to take a small tuck at the corner of each scallop so the braid will conform to the proper shape.

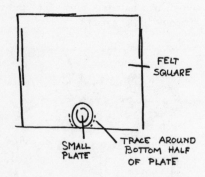

FELT
SQUARE

SMALL
PLATE

TRACE AROUND
BOTTOM HALF
OF PLATE

Continue making scallops in this manner, working from the center toward both corners, until one side has been completed.

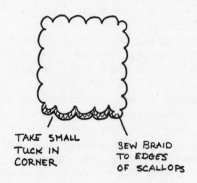

TAKE SMALL
TUCK IN
CORNER

SEW BRAID
TO EDGES
OF SCALLOPS

PARTY APRONS

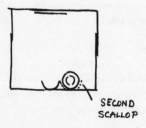

SECOND
SCALLOP

A gala apron with fanciful felt snap-on decorations especially designed for the occasion will add a piquant touch to your party garb. Like a new spring hat, it's guaranteed to lift your spirits and put you in the mood for merriment.

The corner scallop may have to be a little larger or a little smaller than the others to compensate for the remaining fabric.

Change the felt decorations with

the changing seasons and holidays, and voilà! A new apron!

Incidentally, these dainty trifles make welcome gifts for popular hostesses, so why not make a few?

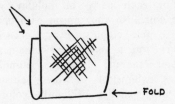

OPEN ENDS

FOLD

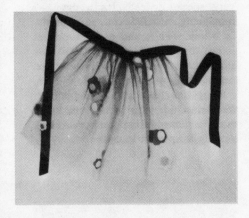

MATERIALS NEEDED:

1 square yard nylon net—any color
2 yards velvet ribbon—the same color as the net
thread—to match the net
needle
10–12 snaps
ruler
scissors
felt—this usually comes in 10-inch squares. The colors you select depend upon the subject matter of the decorations you choose to attach to the apron.
sequins (*optional*)
beads (*optional*)
white glue

DIRECTIONS:

To make the basic apron, begin by folding the net in half.

The fold will form the bottom edge of the apron, and the two open ends will be at the top.

Gather the top of the apron by sewing long running stitches through both thicknesses of the net about 1 inch from the top. Then pull the gathering stitches tight until the top of the apron measures approximately 15 inches.

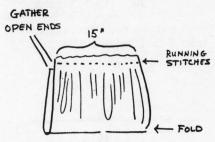

GATHER OPEN ENDS

15"

RUNNING STITCHES

FOLD

Make the waistband by sewing the ribbon to the top of the apron, being sure to hide the gathering stitches behind the ribbon.

The middle of the ribbon should be attached to the middle of the apron so the ties will be the same length.

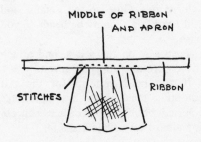

MIDDLE OF RIBBON AND APRON

STITCHES

RIBBON

Now the fun begins!

For each party or holiday you can embellish your apron with decorative felt cutouts. Every occasion offers you a new idea: long-eared Easter rabbits, beaming pumpkin faces, whimsical snowmen, clusters of bright holly, brilliantly colorful fall leaves, gay summer flowers, valentine hearts, Thanksgiving turkeys —these are only a few suggestions. Your imagination is sure to provide you with dozens of others.

In order that the felt designs may be quickly and easily changed, they are attached by sewing snaps to the apron and to the felt cutouts.

About ten or twelve cutouts, scattered casually on the apron, are a good number. Each should be roughly from 1 to 3 inches in size.

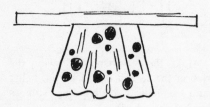

Simply cut out the shape you have decided upon from appropriately colored felt. Glue on felt details, and add sparkling sequins or beads if you wish.

Then sew on the snaps, and attach the decorations to your apron.

If you need patterns for the felt cutouts, magazines or children's coloring books are excellent sources for almost any subject matter.

CIRCUS BIRTHDAY PARTIES FOR CHILDREN

A child's birthday is something very special indeed. It's a day he's impatiently awaited for an eternity (a whole year!), and a milestone of living, loving and learning. So give him a day to remember—till the next one comes around!

Bring the thrill and excitement of the circus into your home with these exuberant decorations, and watch his face light up with wonder.

Clown Centerpiece

This colorful and comical clown is a sure-fire hit with the small fry. His quizzical expression of mirthful woe is an invitation to whoops of laughter. Even grownups will find his infectious gaiety hard to resist!

MATERIALS NEEDED:

1 large round balloon
newspaper
wallpaper paste
1 empty tin can
white glue
scissors
semigloss or flat white enamel
paint brush
turpentine
1 package of crepe paper—any bright color
felt—an assortment of gay colors in 10-inch squares
white cardboard—poster board may be used
stapler

DIRECTIONS:

To make the clown's head, begin by filling the balloon with air and tie the opening shut.

Tear newspaper into 1-inch squares, soak in the wallpaper paste, and mix to a soupy consistency.

Smoothly apply three or four layers of paste-soaked squares until the entire balloon is completely covered.

When this has been done, put the balloon on a tin can to dry for about 24 hours.

Then paint the balloon with white enamel. Use as many coats as necessary to cover the newspaper, letting the enamel dry thoroughly after each coat.

Cut two large ears from cardboard, and attach them to the papier-mâché head with white glue. Hold the ears

in place with several straight pins until the glue sets.

EAR

From white cardboard, cut a large nose, folding it in the middle to make it three-dimensional.

NOSE

Glue this in place, again using straight pins to hold it until the glue sets.

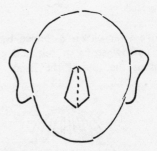

Next, fashion facial details from various colors of felt. For example, cut a big red circle for the tip of the nose, large black eyes with blue pupils, and an oversized red mouth. Add rosy-red cheeks and quizzical black eyebrows. Attach each piece securely to the head with white glue.

To make the neck, cover a tin can with a wide crepe paper ruffle, and glue a large felt polka-dot bow tie near the top of the ruffle.

Give your clown a toupee by cutting narrow strips of felt and gluing them to the top of the head.

Now all he needs is a hat to complete the picture.

Cut a piece of cardboard into a large triangle with a rounded bottom, and roll it into a cone. Use glue or staples to hold it together.

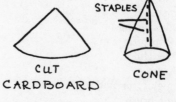

Finish the hat with a crepe paper tassel and a ruffle around the bottom, and trim with felt polka dots.

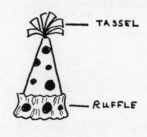

Frivolous Favors

Give each child a clown of his own, and close your ears to the shrill cries of delight. Filled with an assortment of candy, these humorous favors will be an instant success.

MATERIALS NEEDED:

paper or cardboard nut cups—1 for each guest
crepe paper—any color
felt—you will need white, as well as a variety of lively colors
white glue

scissors
cardboard or poster board
stapler
ruler

DIRECTIONS:

Measure and cut a piece of crepe paper large enough to cover the outside of the nut cup.

Ruffle the edges, and attach it to the cup with staples.

Cover a 2×3-inch cardboard rectangle with white glue and white felt.

Then cut an oval shape from the rectangle to make the clown's head.

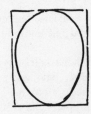

From white felt cut two ears and glue them to either side of the head.

Add a face by cutting the eyes, nose and mouth, etc., from various colors of felt, and glue each piece into place.

Attach a swatch of felt hair and a jaunty hat made of felt to finish

the clown, and glue him to the front of the nut cup.

Party Hats

These clown hats are made to order for sunny smiles and shining faces.

MATERIALS NEEDED:

cardboard or poster board
crepe paper—any color
felt—an assortment of colors
stapler
white glue
scissors
ruler

DIRECTIONS:

From cardboard cut a shape which looks like a triangle with one rounded side. The two straight sides should be about 9 inches long, and the rounded side about 12 inches.

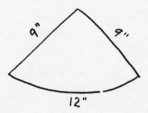

To form the hat, roll the cardboard into a cone and fasten it with staples or glue.

STAPLES

Use glue to trim the hat with a crepe paper tassel and ruffle and varying sizes of felt polka dots.

Clownful Tablecloth

As any child will tell you, ten clowns are funnier than one. This droll tablecloth will provide an ample supply of these laughable jesters.

MATERIALS NEEDED:

felt—white and a number of other
   colors
white glue
scissors
needle
thread
tablecloth—any color to complement
   the clown centerpiece
ruler

DIRECTIONS:

Divide the white felt into six or eight 5-inch squares and cut a large oval shape from each piece to form a head.

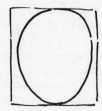

For each head cut two large ears from white felt and attach them with glue.

Then cut facial features from brightly colored felt and glue them in position.

Don't forget his hair!

A polka-dot hat and a ruffle around the neck, both made of felt, give him a properly clownish look.

When the glue is dry, sew the clowns to your tablecloth, using several small stitches.

A circus isn't complete without

balloons, so suspend an extravagant assortment of these to float gracefully above your table.

ADULT BIRTHDAY PARTIES

Make the man in your life king for a day! These resplendent decorations will lend a touch of reality to his castles in Spain and attest to the fact that he is lord and master of all he surveys. He may not admit it, but he'll love the idea—and you for thinking of it!

Imperial Crown Centerpiece

Flashing with the brilliance of molten gold and encrusted with precious gems, this majestic headpiece blazes with imperial beauty. Surrounded with a wreath of fresh flowers or laurel leaves, it's worthy of an emperor—in the grand tradition!

MATERIALS NEEDED:

cardboard or poster board
metallic gold spray paint
white glue
sequins—1 package of assorted colors
scissors
gold braid or rickrack
beads—from an inexpensive necklace
stapler
crystal or china or plastic cake plate

DIRECTIONS:

Begin by drawing and cutting a simple crown shape from a cardboard rectangle, 8 inches wide and 22 inches long.

Cut several diamond-shaped and triangular openings in the front of the crown shape.

Then bend the two ends of cardboard and staple them together at the back to make the crown.

Spray the crown with several coats of metallic gold paint, letting it dry after each coat.

When the final coat has dried, embellish the crown generously with gold braid, sequins, dazzling beads or pearls. Use white glue to hold these in place.

Elevate the crown by putting it on a cake plate, and surround it with a wreath of fresh flowers or green leaves. If a plastic cake plate is used, it should be painted gold to complete the royal effect.

Majestic Favors

As a mark of royal favor, distribute these glittering treasure chests among his majesty's loyal subjects. Filled with candies wrapped in gold foil, they're worth a king's ransom.

MATERIALS NEEDED:

small empty cardboard boxes—1 for each guest, about the size used to box costume jewelry
metallic gold spray paint
white glue
multicolored beads
sequins—a mixture of colors
gold braid or rickrack

DIRECTIONS:

To make a miniature treasure chest, simply spray a small cardboard box, inside and out, with metallic gold paint.

When this is dry, apply a second coat if necessary, and let it dry again.

Glue gold braid around the sides of the box, and an elaborate arrangement of beads and sequins to the cover.

Loving Cup Candleholders

Add to the royal regalia with these gem-studded loving cups.

MATERIALS NEEDED:

2 inexpensive parfait glasses
metallic gold spray paint
4 strips of cardboard—each piece should be ½ inch wide and 7 inches long
white glue
gold braid or rickrack
sequins
beads
2 candles—a color of your choice

DIRECTIONS:

Make one candleholder by gluing two cardboard strips to the sides of the glass to form the handles of a loving cup.

Then attach two cardboard handles to the other glass in the same manner.

When the glue has set, spray the glasses with gold paint. Let this dry, and spray paint again.

After the second coat of paint has dried, glue luminous beads to the base and top rim of each glass.

Add decorative gold braid and sequins to the sides of each loving cup, and insert your choice of candles.

JUST-FOR-FUN CHILDREN'S PARTIES

Like unexpected gifts, children's parties given "just for fun" are often the most successful.

They afford special delight, because there's no particular reason for them —except lots of love!

Zoo Centerpiece

A kittenish tiger, a roly-poly panda or a smiling giraffe will look right at home in this quick and clever centerpiece. Make it large enough to accommodate one or more of our furry friends and provide high adventure for children of all ages.

And since you're featuring the zoo citizens, why not distribute animal crackers as favors? They're certain to produce excited shouts of recognition!

MATERIALS NEEDED:

empty cardboard box—at least 12 inches high, wide and deep. Use a size that will fit in the center of your table.
enamel spray paint—flat, semigloss or gloss, in a color of your choice
scissors
pencil
knife
construction paper or felt—something very colorful. It should be 4 inches longer and 4 inches wider than the top of the box.
straight pins
white glue
ruler
thick yarn—1 yard of 4 or 5 different colors
1 or more stuffed animals—small enough to fit inside the box

DIRECTIONS:

You will need a box that has four sides and a top. If there is a bottom to the box, use scissors or a knife to remove it.

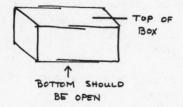

To form the bars of the cage, cut out three or four rectangular shapes on each of the four sides of the box. Each cardboard strip or bar that is left should be about 1 or 2 inches wide.

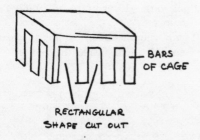

Then paint the cage, inside and out, with the spray enamel.

When the paint has dried, give the cage a second coat if necessary, and dry again.

Next, make a canopy for the top of the cage from construction paper or felt.

Measure the top of the box, and cut the felt or paper to these measurements.

Cover the top of the box with the paper or felt, gluing it securely in place.

From the leftover strips of felt or paper, cut four 2-inch strips, one for each side of the box.

Scallop one side of each strip, and glue the strips to the sides of the cage, directly under the top of the box.

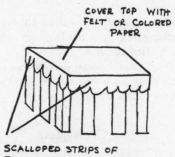

Add some bright foolery to the canopy with extra thick yarn of various colors.

Tie a knot approximately 1 inch from the end of one piece of yarn. Fluff out the remaining inch of yarn to make a tassel.

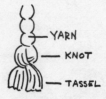

Attach the knot to one side of the canopy with glue, using a straight pin to hold it in place until the glue has set.

Pull the yarn taut across the top of the box to the opposite side of the canopy.

Trim the yarn to the correct length, allowing for another knot and tassel, and glue this side in place, too. Continue making yarn streamers and glue them every 2 inches across the

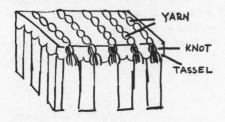

canopy. Place the animals in their cage, and you're ready for a party!

Train Centerpiece

There's something endlessly fascinating about toy trains—even adults can't resist them!

This boldly imaginative centerpiece looks complicated, but it's surprisingly easy to construct.

NOTE: For a realistic touch, fill the car behind the locomotive with coal-black jellybeans or licorice chunks.

MATERIALS NEEDED:

empty oatmeal box and cover
cardboard tube—from the middle of a waxed paper roll or something similar
black felt or construction paper— about 10 square inches
small wooden spool—minus the thread
black spray enamel—flat, semigloss or gloss
colored spray enamel—a color to contrast with the black; flat, semi-gloss or gloss
white glue
straight pins
scissors
small box and cover—the box that baby shoes or children's shoes come in is perfect. This is smaller than a regular shoe box.
cardboard—poster board is fine

empty box—about 6 inches long, 6 inches wide and 4 inches high. This will be used to make the coal car.

ruler

knife

decorative braid and ball fringe (*optional*)

DIRECTIONS:

Begin making the locomotive by gluing one side of the oatmeal box, with its cover on, to the top of the shoe box cover. Be generous with the glue to ensure sturdy construction.

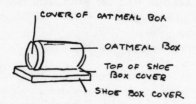

Then glue the bottom of the shoe box to the bottom of the oatmeal box. This will become the cab of the locomotive when finished.

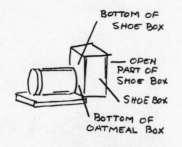

Next, construct a sunshade for the top of the cab from a piece of cardboard or poster board.

Measure the width of the top of the cab. Then measure the distance from the front to the back of the cab, and add 3 extra inches to allow for an overhang.

Place the piece of cardboard on top of the cab so that 1 inch extends in front of the cab and 2 inches extend in the back.

Then fold down 1 inch in front and 1 inch in back, and glue the shade in place.

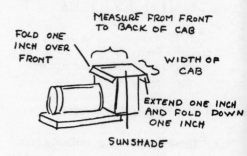

SUNSHADE

When the glue has set, use the colored enamel you have selected to spray paint the locomotive and the empty box to be used for the coal car. Let the paint dry, spray with a second coat, and dry again.

While the paint is drying, make cardboard wheels for the train by cutting out eight circles which are each 1 inch in diameter, and two circles which are 3 inches in diameter.

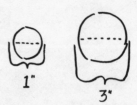

With a knife, cut a 3-inch section from the cardboard tube to make the smokestack.

Fabricate a bumper for the front of the locomotive from a piece of cardboard, following the pattern provided, and fold the bumper lightly in the middle.

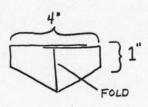

FOLD

Spray paint all of the wheels, the smokestack, the wooden spool, and the bumper with black paint. Let this dry, and apply a second coat.

When everything has dried completely, you're ready to begin to assemble the train.

Attach four of the smaller wheels to the coal car by poking a straight pin through the center of each wheel, and then pushing the pin firmly into the bottom of the box.

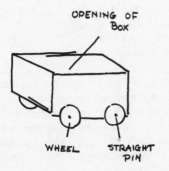

OPENING OF BOX

WHEEL   STRAIGHT PIN

Glue the cardboard tube to the top of the oatmeal box, approximately 1½ inches from the front.

Secure the wooden spool to the center of the oatmeal box cover with glue.

Then attach the bumper to the front of the shoe box cover, using straight pins and glue.

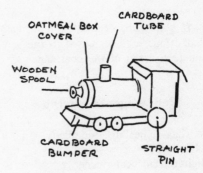

OATMEAL BOX COVER   CARDBOARD TUBE

WOODEN SPOOL

CARDBOARD BUMPER   STRAIGHT PIN

Attach two of the small wheels to one side of the locomotive, placing the first wheel approximately ½ inch from the front of the shoe box cover.

Put a pin through the center of each wheel, and then push the pin firmly into the box cover. A dab of glue on the back of the wheel will help keep it steady.

Fasten one large wheel to the bottom of the cab, again using straight pins and glue to hold it in place.

In a like manner, affix the remaining wheels to the other side of the locomotive.

Complete the train by cutting three rectangular windows for the cab from black felt or construction paper. Each should be approximately 2×3 inches.

Glue one window to each side of the cab and one across the front.

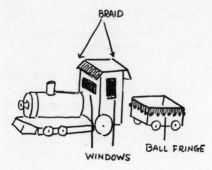

BRAID

BALL FRINGE

WINDOWS

If you wish, decorative braid and ball fringe may be added to the sunshade and rim of the coal car.

Red Wagon Centerpiece

The appealing simplicity of a child's red wagon is reflected in this lighthearted centerpiece.

Piled high with colorfully wrapped gifts, favors, an assortment of toy animals or dolls, it's as gay as a yard full of tulips!

MATERIALS NEEDED:

empty cardboard box—a box approximately 3 inches high, 12 inches wide and 16 inches long is a good size, although a larger or smaller box may be used if you wish. (A taller box can be used by cutting the sides down.)
red enamel—gloss, semigloss or flat enamel. Spray paint or regular brushing enamel may be used.
black enamel—gloss, semigloss or flat enamel. Spray paint or regular brushing enamel may be used.
fairly heavy cardboard—cut apart another box for the needed cardboard
white glue
masking tape

4 small nails or thumbtacks
scissors or knife
pencil
ruler
paint brush—if you are using brushing enamel
turpentine—to clean the brush

DIRECTIONS:

The cardboard box, which is approximately $16 \times 12 \times 3$ inches, will be the basic structure of the wagon. If you are using a smaller or a larger box, the size of the wheels and the handle will have to be altered slightly to allow for the difference in dimensions.

Begin by painting the box red. Let the paint dry, give it a second coat, and let it dry again.

To construct the wheels, cut four circles from fairly heavy cardboard. Each circle should be 5 inches in diameter. Use scissors or a knife to sever the cardboard, whichever seems to work better.

Next, cut one 30×20-inch cardboard strip. Cut a second piece of cardboard measuring 1×5 inches. These will be used to make the handle for the wagon.

Use black enamel to paint both sides of the four wheels and the two pieces of cardboard to be used for the handle. Let this dry, and apply a second coat if necessary.

When everything is thoroughly dry, you're ready to begin building your wagon.

Push a small nail or thumbtack through the middle of one wheel. Spread a 1-inch circle of glue around the nail on the back of the wheel. Then push the nail, with the wheel on it, firmly into the red cardboard box. The wheel should be placed so that the nail goes into the bottom edge of the box.

Allow for at least 2 inches between the wheel and the corner of the box.

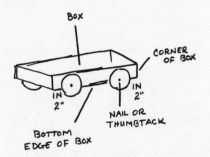

BOX
CORNER OF BOX
IN 2"
IN 2"
NAIL OR THUMBTACK
BOTTOM EDGE OF BOX

To make a handle for the wagon, first glue the 1×5-inch piece of cardboard across one end of the 3× 20-inch cardboard strip to form the top of the handle.

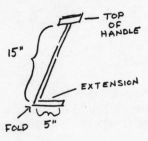

1X5 INCH CARDBOARD
3X20 INCH STRIP

Then make a fold in the longer strip 15 inches from the top of the handle.

This will leave a 5-inch extension at the other end to be attached to the underside of the wagon.

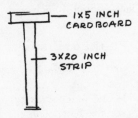

TOP OF HANDLE
15"
EXTENSION
FOLD 5"

Let 3 inches of the extension show from beneath the wagon. Use glue and masking tape to secure the remaining 2 inches to the underside at the front of the wagon.

FOLD 3"

Now heap the wagon with an assortment of tempting and colorful items, and it's ready for the table!

BRIDAL SHOWERS

Frothy, frilly, feminine and frankly sentimental—that's the only way to describe a bridal shower! Match the mood of the radiant bride-to-be with these gala shower decorations.

Sparkling Sprinkler Centerpiece

Brimful of flowers and decked out with lace, this flashing and totally

feminine centerpiece is a real attention-getter.

Miniature Sprinklers

Favor your guests with these dainty miniatures.

MATERIALS NEEDED:

1 large plastic or metal watering can
metallic gold spray paint
white lace—about 2 inches wide and
   1 yard long
gold rickrack or braid
velvet ribbon—about 1½ inches wide
   and 1 yard long
scissors
white glue
flowers—real or plastic. Use one
   color or several colors, and enough
   flowers to make a pleasing arrangement.

MATERIALS NEEDED:

cardboard nut cups
lightweight cardboard
1 box of paper or plastic drinking
   straws
metallic gold spray paint
white glue
scissors
small buttons—(1 for each sprinkler.)
   Buy those with 2 or 4 holes in
   them to be used for the water
   spout.
velvet ribbon—¼ inch wide, to
   match the ribbon on your centerpiece. You will need about 12
   inches of ribbon for each favor.
gold rickrack or braid
white lace—about 1 inch wide

DIRECTIONS:

Spray the watering can with gold paint. Let it dry, and apply a second coat.

When this is dry, glue lace, gold rickrack or braid around the top and bottom of the can.

As a graceful gesture, tie a large velvet bow in the center of the top handle on the can.

DIRECTIONS:

To make one sprinkler, begin by cutting two strips of cardboard, ½ inch wide and 4 inches long.

To make the handle on the top of the sprinkler, glue 1 strip of cardboard to both sides of the nut cup, arching it across the top of the cup.

Now fill the can with your selection of real or plastic flowers.

Use the other strip of cardboard to make a handle on the back of the sprinkler. Glue one end of the strip to the outside of the cup near the bottom. The other end should be glued to the top of the cup on the inside.

With scissors, make a hole in the front of the cup, centering it evenly.

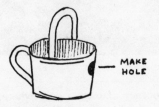

MAKE HOLE

Cut 2 inches from a drinking straw and insert this into the hole to form the water spout. About 1 inch of the straw should be pushed through the hole and glued to the inside of the cup.

Attach a small button to the end of the straw with glue.

When the glue has set, spray the sprinkler with gold paint and let it dry.

Then trim the outside of the cup with lace, rickrack or braid and velvet ribbon to match the centerpiece.

Gold Lace Candleholders

Candlelight will heighten the romantic atmosphere and flatter your guests. Use these ornamental candleholders to add a finishing festive look to your table.

MATERIALS NEEDED:

inexpensive clear glass candleholders
metallic gold spray paint
white glue
scissors
white lace—about 1 inch wide
flowers—to match those in your centerpiece
tall candles—a complementary color

DIRECTIONS:

Spray the candleholders with gold paint and let them dry.

Glue lace around the sides of each candleholder to give them a delicate look.

Place the candles in the holders, and arrange flowers tastefully around the base of each candle.

Preserved Flowers

Your guest of honor will be rapturous when you present her with this souvenir of lasting beauty. A cherished memento, these flowers will always remind her of the happiest time of her life.

MATERIALS NEEDED:

sugar flowers—from the cake
white semigloss spray enamel

DIRECTIONS:

Remove the sugar flowers from the cake, being careful to keep them intact.

Place the flowers on waxed paper and let them set until the sugar is dry and very hard. They should be left standing for a month or more to permit the sugar to dry thoroughly.

Then spray the flowers with the white enamel, and let them dry. To give them the look of fine china and preserve them permanently, you should apply at least ten coats of white enamel, letting each coat dry before applying the next. Be sure to spray the underside of the flowers, too.

Use this method to preserve the flowers from a wedding cake. This would be a unique gift for newly-weds.

BABY SHOWERS

A shower for a lady-in-waiting always carries an air of pleasurable anticipation. These decorations will herald the coming of the new arrival with a suitably joyful flourish.

Angel Centerpiece

Use this lovable angel to grace your table and typify the cherubic

innocence of infants everywhere. Her sugar-'n'-spice look will win the hearts of all your guests.

MATERIALS NEEDED:

1 empty bottle—this will be used to make the body of the angel. A Windex bottle has about the right shape for this.
flexible wire
1 small white styrofoam ball—to be used for the head
cardboard or poster board
wallpaper paste
newspaper
semigloss white spray enamel
pink, blue and black hobby enamel—
   1 small bottle of each
1 fine paint brush
turpentine
silver or gold braid
pink and blue felt—1 square of each
white glue
scissors
ruler

stapler
wire cutters
Treasure Gold Wax Gilt
blue net—¼ yard

DIRECTIONS:

Mix the wallpaper paste with water until it's fairly thick, and tear newspaper into small squares.

Cover the entire bottle with two layers of paste-soaked squares. Be sure to smooth each square carefully in place with your fingers.

To form the arms of the angel, cut a 20-inch piece of wire. Make a loop in the middle of the wire and slip it over the neck of the bottle, pulling the ends of the wire to tighten the loop.

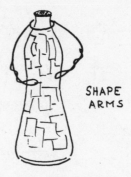

SHAPE ARMS

Tear a strip of newspaper approximately 2 inches wide and 12 inches long and soak it in wallpaper paste.

Then wind the strip loosely around the wire arm, starting at the hand and ending at what should be the shoulder. This will be a sleeve of her gown.

Attach the sleeve to the shoulder with small paste-soaked squares of newspaper.

Make the other sleeve the same way.

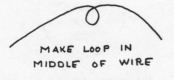

MAKE LOOP IN MIDDLE OF WIRE

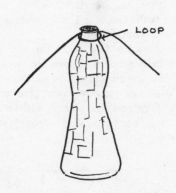

LOOP

WIND STRIP AROUND ARM

To finish the neck, cover the wire loop with small pieces of newspaper soaked in paste.

Next, cut two wings from cardboard and attach them to the back of the angel with small strips of newspaper which have been soaked in paste. The wings should be proportioned to fit the size of your bottle.

Bend both ends of the wire forward in a gentle curve to shape the arms, and make a small loop at the end of each arm for the hands.

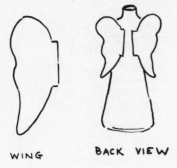

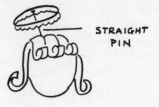

STRAIGHT PIN

WING   BACK VIEW

Cover the wings with one or two layers of paste-soaked squares to make them stiff and prevent drooping.

Make the head by covering a small styrofoam ball with newspaper squares which have been soaked in paste, and affix the ball to the neck of the bottle, using white glue.

Use narrow strips of paste-soaked newspaper for the hair. Make a small curl at the end of each strip and attach it to the head.

When you have finished the hair, put the angel away until the papier-mâché is completely dry.

Then paint her with white spray enamel. Let this dry, and apply a second coat. Be sure to get paint into all the small creases and folds.

After the paint has dried, make a halo from gold or silver braid, attaching it to her head with a straight pin, so it appears to hover above her head.

Decorate the neck, sleeves and hem of her gown with silver or gold braid, using glue to hold it in place.

Paint small stars on her dress and wings with pink and blue enamel.

Give her a face by using black enamel to shape her brows, lashes, eyes and nose. Then use the pink enamel for her mouth, and the blue for the pupils of her eyes.

Let the enamel dry and add golden highlights to her hair, wings and gown with Treasure Gold, dabbing it on with your fingers.

Now make felt stars for her to hold in her hands. Begin by cutting out two 2-inch squares of cardboard.

Cover one square with glue and pink felt, and the other with blue felt. Cut one star shape from each square.

Make a small hole in the bottom of each star, and insert a short wire stem.

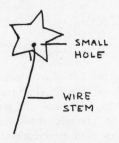

SMALL HOLE

WIRE STEM

Place the stars in her hands, bending the wire stems around the hands to keep them firmly in place.

Finally, make a fluffy blue net cloud. Pleat and gather the net until you have made a complete circle. Staple it in the middle several times to hold it together, and place it gently beneath her feet.

STAPLES

Fantasy Favors

Smiles will greet the appearance of these ingenious nut or candy cups created to match your centerpiece.

MATERIALS NEEDED:

cardboard or paper nut cups
pink and blue felt
cardboard or poster board
flexible wire
masking tape
gold or silver braid
wallpaper paste
newspaper
semigloss white spray enamel
pink and blue hobby enamel—1 small
   bottle of each
fine paint brush
turpentine
blue net—1 2×10-inch piece for each
   nut cup
scissors
white glue
wire cutters

DIRECTIONS:

Tear the newspaper into small squares and soak in wallpaper paste.

Cover each nut cup with two layers of paste-soaked squares and let the papier-mâché dry.

Spray the cups with white enamel. Several coats may be needed to cover the newspaper.

When the paint has dried, glue silver or gold braid around the top and bottom of each cup, and paint small pink and blue stars on the sides to match the angel.

Then cut one 2-inch square of cardboard for each favor, and cover these with glue and pink or blue felt.

From each square cut a star shape, and make a small hole in the bottom of each star.

Insert a 6-inch wire stem into the hole, and bend one end of the wire to hold the star firmly. Attach the other end of the wire to the bottom of the nut cup with masking tape.

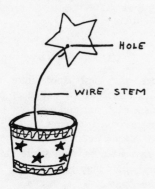

HOLE

WIRE STEM

Line the inside of the cup with a blue net cloud, and fill it with nuts or candies.

Heavenly Tablecloth

Put your angel right at home with a star-studded tablecloth. It's perfectly tailored for her!

MATERIALS NEEDED:

white, pink or blue tablecloth
pink and blue felt—two 10-inch squares of each color
white glue
scissors
pink and blue thread—1 spool of each
needle

DIRECTIONS:

Divide the felt into 5-inch squares and cut one large star from each square. Six blue and six pink stars should be enough, depending upon the size of your tablecloth.

5" SQUARE

Trim the edges of each star by gluing gold or silver braid to the felt.

Then use matching thread to attach the corners of each star to your tablecloth. These can be removed easily when you wish- to launder the cloth.

Starry Candleholders

Bring the silvery glimmer of the wishing star to your table with these twinkling candleholders.

MATERIALS NEEDED:

clear glass candleholders
pink and blue felt
flexible wire
wire cutters

white glue
scissors
stapler
florist clay
semigloss white spray enamel
cardboard
blue net—a piece 3×15 inches for
  each candleholder
candles—pink, blue or white

DIRECTIONS:

Paint the candleholders with spray enamel and let them dry. Then fill the bottom of each candleholder with florist clay, and insert the candles.

Make a blue cloud for each candleholder by folding and gathering a 3×15-inch piece of net into a complete circle. This may be held together with staples or blue thread.

Place the net circle around the base of the candle to hide the florist clay in the bottom of the holder.

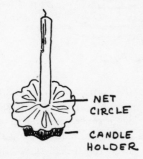

Cut out five 2-inch cardboard squares for each candleholder, and

cover them first with glue and then with pink and blue felt. From each square cut one star shape.

Make a small hole at the bottom of each star, and insert a short wire stem.

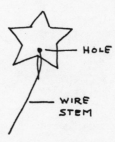

Finally, push the stems through the net into the florist clay so the stars will encircle the candles.

ANNIVERSARY PARTIES

A wedding anniversary is a time for remembering and for rejoicing;

for teasing and for tenderness; for laughing and for loving.

Whether the party's for two or two hundred, these festive decorations will help to make the occasion as joyous and as memorable as the event it commemorates.

Wedding Cake Centerpiece

The original cake may have long since vanished, but this romantically realistic centerpiece will evoke its image. Radiant with flowers and sparkling with lace, it looks like a confectioner's dream!

MATERIALS NEEDED:

1 package small white paper doilies—
about 6 inches in diameter
spray enamel—choose silver for the twenty-fifth anniversary, gold for the fiftieth, a pastel color in gloss, semigloss or flat enamel for any other year
florist clay or child's modeling clay
2 yards narrow lace—about ½ inch wide; buy an inexpensive lace

3 yards wide lace—approximately 2 inches wide
cardboard or poster board will work; 1 or 2 6-inch squares
pencil
white glue
scissors
paper towels
1 yard white satin ribbon—½ or 1 inch wide
artificial lily of the valley—1 small bunch
40 small artificial flowers—any small flower, such as a rose, will do; select white or pastel colors
3 empty round containers—these will be used to make a three-tiered cake, so the containers should be three different sizes. A large round hat box is perfect for the bottom layer. Any plastic, cardboard or metal container can be used.

DIRECTIONS:

Stack the three round containers one on top of the other, putting the largest on the bottom and the smallest on the top.

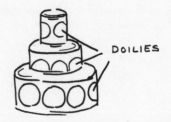

Trim the sides of each container with paper doilies, using a whole or a half of a doily, depending upon the size of the container. Use a damp paper towel to spread glue lightly on the back of each doily so it will adhere to the container.

Add lace to each tier of the cake

by gluing one or two rows of lace around the sides of each container. Alternate the narrow and the wide lace for variety.

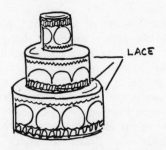

LACE

When the glue has set, spray paint the cake with the enamel you have selected. Let the paint dry, give it a second coat, and let it dry again.

To make the number or numbers designating the anniversary year to be used on the top of the cake, you will need one 6-inch square of cardboard for each number. For example, if it is the fifth anniversary, you will need 1 square, and if it's the twenty-fifth, you will need two.

Glue a paper doily to the front and back of each cardboard square.

When the glue has dried, draw the number on the doily-covered cardboard. Make the number as large as you can, keeping it within the perimeter of the doily.

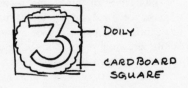

DOILY

CARDBOARD SQUARE

Cut the number out of the cardboard, and spray paint it on both sides to match the cake.

After the paint is dry, attach the numbers to the top of the cake. Use a small ball of florist clay or child's modeling clay placed on the bottom of the number to hold it erect.

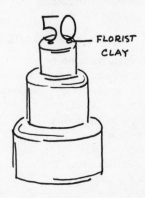

FLORIST CLAY

Arrange sprigs of lily of the valley around the numbers. Each sprig should radiate out from the center of the top of the cake, right under the numbers. Use a little clay to hold each stem in place.

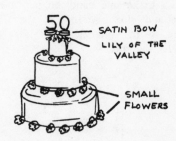

SATIN BOW
LILY OF THE VALLEY
SMALL FLOWERS

Then add a gleaming white satin bow to hide the stems and florist clay.

Cut the stems of the 40 artificial flowers so that only a ½-inch stem remains. Surround the bottom of each tier of the cake with the tiny flowers. These may be attached with a dab of glue or a little clay, or they may be simply left loose.

Champagne Candleholders

Use glimmering crystal and frosty lace to accent your candles and set the mood for dreaming.

MATERIALS NEEDED:

2 inexpensive wine or parfait glasses
florist clay or child's modeling clay
2 tall candles—to complement the color of the cake
2 white paper doilies
white glue
scissors
1 yard wide lace—the same as used on the cake
1 yard narrow lace—the same as used on the cake
spray enamel—the same paint that was used for the cake
tape measure
paper towels

DIRECTIONS:

To make one candleholder, measure and glue one row of the wide lace to the side of one glass just under the rim.

CANDLE
WIDE LACE
DOILY
NARROW LACE

Then attach two rows of narrow lace to the bottom of the glass, just above the stem.

Decorate the sides of the glass between the rows of lace with paper doilies.

Cut the doilies into small pieces to fit the empty spaces on the glass, and glue them in place. Use damp paper towels to spread the glue evenly on the back of the doilies.

Fashion the second candleholder in the same manner.

When the glue has set, spray paint both of the glasses to match the cake centerpiece. Let the paint dry, apply another coat, and dry again.

Then insert the candles, holding them securely in place with florist clay or child's modeling clay.

Lacelike Place Mats or Tablecloth

Sprinkled with the delicate tracery of snowflakes, these graceful table coverings have a truly bridal appearance.

MATERIALS NEEDED:

spray paint—the same which was used for the centerpiece
paper doily
white tablecloth or place mats—use a sheet or ready-made tablecloth, or fabric or paper place mats. White drawing paper can be used to make inexpensive place mats.

DIRECTIONS:

Select either white place mats or a white tablecloth to be painted. NOTE: The enamel won't wash out,

so don't use one of your favorite tablecloths!

Medium-weight, 12×18-inch white drawing paper is excellent for making inexpensive place mats which can be thrown away after they are used.

Lay the doily on the tablecloth or place mat.

Hold the can of spray paint about 12 inches away from the doily, and then pretend that you are trying to paint the doily. Do this quickly, so just a light coat of paint covers the doily. You'll find when you remove the doily that there is a delicate design left on the tablecloth or place mat where the paint went through the holes and around the edges of the doily.

It might be a good plan to practice this technique on some old newspaper until you get the hang of it before trying it on your tablecloth.

Use this procedure to scatter designs over your tablecloth or place mats. If you prefer, the designs may be arranged in a formal pattern.

Let the paint dry overnight, and it's party time!

BON VOYAGE PARTY

A bon voyage party holds a promise of both pain and pleasure, for it's always hard to say good-bye, if only for a little while.

Send the travelers off in grand style with a party designed to ease the pain of parting, and provide them with a happy, heart-warming memory of those they left behind.

Ship Centerpiece

Whatever their port of call, your guests will be entranced by this gallant little craft.

Afloat on a sea of flowers, she brings with her visions of enchanted isles and exotic ports, of calm, star-studded nights and golden days sparkling with romance, mystery and adventure.

MATERIALS NEEDED:

white cardboard—poster board or any medium-weight cardboard

empty cardboard box—without a cover; approximately 18 inches long, 6 inches wide and 3 inches deep

empty cardboard box or box cover—about 8 inches long, 5 inches wide and 1 inch deep

felt—3 or 4 bright colors. You will need 1 10-inch square of each color.

pencil

white glue

scissors

ruler

empty cardboard tube—from the middle of a waxed paper or aluminum foil roll knife

spray can cover—like that found on a Windex spray can or a hair spray can

large wooden spool—minus the thread; or something similar in size and shape

10 inches of ¼-inch doweling

12 inches of lightweight chain or twine

black enamel
white or other
light-colored
enamel
} Either spray paint or brushing enamel. Gloss, semi-gloss or flat enamel.

paint brush—if you are using brushing enamel

turpentine—to clean the brush

straight pins

DIRECTIONS:

The hull of the ship will be constructed from the larger empty box.

Begin by neatly cutting away one end of the box with scissors or a knife, whichever works better.

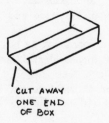

CUT AWAY ONE END OF BOX

Then starting at the cut-away end of the box, make a 6-inch-long slit along the bottom edge on both sides of the box.

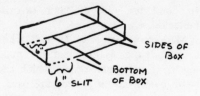

SIDES OF BOX

BOTTOM OF BOX

6" SLIT

Pull the two sides of the box together until they meet, forming the point of the hull at the front of the ship.

Use glue and straight pins to secure the point, removing the pins when the glue has set.

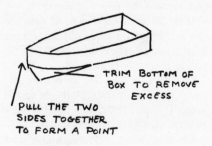

TRIM BOTTOM OF BOX TO REMOVE EXCESS

PULL THE TWO SIDES TOGETHER TO FORM A POINT

When you have drawn the front of the ship together, there will be a small portion of the bottom of the box that will remain on the outside of the point. Use scissors to trim away this excess so the bottom of the box will conform to the new shape.

Use a little glue to hold the bottom of the box to the point of the hull.

Next, using a knife, cut two 3½-inch and one 2½-inch segments from the empty cardboard tube. These will be used to make the smokestacks for the ship.

Draw the shape of an anchor on a 2-inch cardboard square. Cut out the anchor and make a small hole through the top with a paper punch or the point of the scissors.

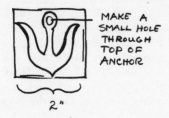

MAKE A
SMALL HOLE
THROUGH
TOP OF
ANCHOR

2"

The hull of the ship, the anchor, the three smokestacks, the 10-inch piece of doweling and the wooden spool should be painted with two coats of black paint. Be sure to let the paint dry thoroughly between coats.

When the second coat of paint has dried, prepare the deck of the ship. Do this by laying the hull of the ship upside down on a piece of white cardboard.

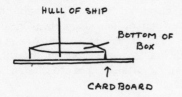

HULL OF SHIP

BOTTOM OF
BOX

↑
CARDBOARD

Then, with a pencil, trace around the shape of the hull and cut out this shape.

TRACE SHAPE
OF HULL

To hold the deck in place, apply glue generously around the upper edges of the hull.

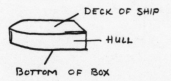

DECK OF SHIP

HULL

BOTTOM OF BOX

Next, paint the small cardboard box or box cover and the spray can cover with the light-colored enamel you have selected. Apply two coats of paint, letting each dry after an application.

To make portholes for the ship, cut twelve small circles from felt of one color, and ten-larger circles from felt of a different color. The small circles should be about the size of a penny, the larger ones the size of a quarter.

Trim each smokestack with one or more bright felt stripes glued in place. Vary the width of the stripes, making some about ¾ inch wide and others a bit narrower.

FELT
STRIPES

To make a bon voyage flag for the ship, cover both sides of a 6×3-inch piece of cardboard first with glue, and then felt.

After the glue has set, cut the shape of a banner from the felt-covered cardboard.

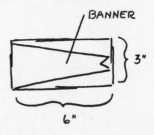

BANNER

} 3"

6"

From felt of a contrasting color, cut out the letters to spell the words BON VOYAGE. Be sure that the letters are sized correctly to fit the flag. Then glue the letters into place on the banner.

When you have completed the flag, glue it to one end of the 10-inch piece of doweling.

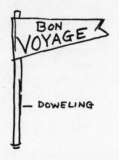

Now the fun of assembling your ship is all that remains.

First, turn the small cardboard box upside down and glue it to the deck of the ship, centering it as much as possible.

Next, glue six of the small portholes to each side of the small cardboard box.

Then glue five of the large portholes to each side of the hull, placing the first one about 7 inches from the front of the ship, and then spacing the others evenly toward the back of the ship.

Center and glue the wooden spool to the front deck of the ship.

Glue the 2½-inch smokestack and one 3½-inch smokestack to the top of the small cardboard box.

Make a ¼-inch hole in the small cardboard box approximately 1 inch from the back of the box, and push the flagpole into this hole.

Then glue the spray can cover and the remaining smokestack to the back deck.

Attach the anchor to one end of the chain or twine. Then affix the other end of the chain or twine to the edge of the deck, approximately 4 inches from the front of the ship, using a straight pin to fasten it securely.

Make a small loop in the chain, and attach this to the deck about 2 inches from the front of the ship, again using a straight pin to hold it in place.

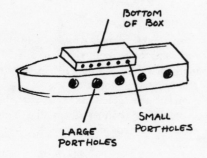

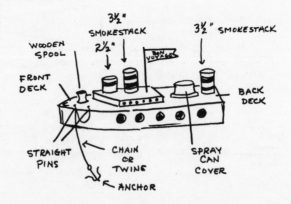

Now launch your ship on an ocean of fresh or artificial flowers or a lake of green leaves, or use it just as it is in the center of your table.

Incidentally, to carry through the party theme completely, try adding maps and travel posters to your walls.

Smokestack Candleholders

Firmly anchored beside your ship, these trim candleholders have an extremely neat and nautical appearance.

MATERIALS NEEDED:

2 empty tin cans—about 5 inches tall and 2 inches in diameter
felt—the same colors used on the ship
white glue
scissors
florist clay or child's modeling clay
enamel—use the black or the lighter color selected for the ship
2 tall candles—in a complementary color

DIRECTIONS:

Remove all labels, and then paint the tin cans inside and out with two coats of enamel. Let the paint dry thoroughly after each application.

Glue three or four felt stripes to the sides of each can. Use felt of several different colors, and vary the width of the stripes.

When the glue has set, place the candles in the smokestack holders, securing them with a bit of florist clay.

Boat Favors

Flags flying, these brave little boats can double as place cards. Fill them with candy Life Savers or nuts to provide your guests with appropriately seafaring souvenirs.

Even a landlubber will find these easy to construct!

MATERIALS NEEDED:

small empty cardboard boxes—1 for each guest; approximately 6 inches long, 2 inches wide and 1 inch high. You will not need the covers.
felt—the colors used for the centerpiece
enamel—2 colors. You can use the same paint that was used on the large ship.
large wooden spool—1 for each boat
cardboard—poster board or a medium-weight cardboard
white pipe cleaners—1 for each boat
florist clay
pencil
white glue
scissors
straight pins
ruler
wood doweling—you will need 1 piece that is 3 inches long and ¾ inch in diameter for each boat.

DIRECTIONS:

The hull for each boat favor will be made following the same directions as those used for the ship centerpiece, but on a smaller scale.

With scissors, cut away one end of the box.

Starting at the cut-away end of the box, make a 2-inch slit along the bottom edge on both sides of the box.

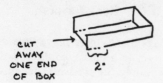

CUT
AWAY
ONE END
OF BOX   2"

Then pull the two sides together to form the pointed front of the hull, joining it with glue and straight pins.

Be sure to trim off any excess cardboard that sticks out from under the front of the boat.

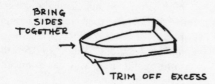

BRING
SIDES
TOGETHER

TRIM OFF EXCESS

When the glue has set, paint the box with two coats of enamel, letting it dry after each application.

Use enamel of another color to paint the wooden spool and the 3-inch piece of doweling, and let this dry.

Next, cut out eight dime-sized portholes from gaily colored felt.

Now construct a small flag to be used as a name tag.

Cover a 1½ × 3-inch piece of cardboard with glue and then with felt. Let the glue dry, and then cut the shape of a banner from the felt-covered cardboard.

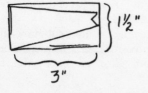

1½"

3"

From felt of a contrasting color, cut letters to spell out the name of one of your guests. Be sure that the letters are scaled to the correct dimensions to fit the flag. Attach the letters to the flag with glue.

Then make a flagpole from a 4-inch piece of pipe cleaner, gluing the completed banner to one end of the pipe cleaner.

LYNN

PIPE
CLEANER

Add two felt stripes to the sides of the doweling smokestack, and you're ready for the final stages of construction.

Evenly space and glue four portholes to each side of the boat.

Put the spool and the doweling erect inside the box, and glue them to the bottom of the box.

DOWELING

SPOOL

LYNN

Place them approximately in the center of the boat, with the spool in front of the doweling.

Finally, attach the flagpole to the bottom of the box, directly behind the doweling, with a small ball of florist clay.

SPECIAL DAY PARTIES

There are certain occasions which just naturally seem to call for an all-out celebration.

Give a champagne sparkle to the day, and add to the general air of madcap merriment with these fresh 'n' fancy decorations.

VALENTINE'S DAY PARTIES

These Valentine's Day decorations are guaranteed to melt the hardest heart.

Hearts and Flowers Centerpiece

What better way to say, "Will you be my Valentine?" than with these charming valentine flowers?

MATERIALS NEEDED:

1 large clay flower pot
styrofoam—to fit the inside of the pot
lightweight cardboard
white glue
flexible wire
wire cutters
florist tape
felt—red and white
red and white checked fabric (*optional;* if you use this, you will need about ¼ yard)
rickrack, braid or lace (*optional;* any color may be used)
red velvet ribbon—to trim the flower pot; 1 inch wide and about 1½ yards long
scissors
semigloss white enamel
paint brush
turpentine

DIRECTIONS:

Begin by painting the flowerpot inside and out with white enamel.

While this is drying, cut out six 4-inch squares and six 2½-inch squares of lightweight cardboard. The number of squares may be increased to make more flowers.

Cut the felt (or fabric) to fit the cardboard squares. You will need two pieces of felt for each square of cardboard.

Spread glue evenly on one side of the cardboard and cover it with a felt square.

Now cover the other side with felt of a contrasting color.

When all of the squares have been covered, let the glue set until dry.

Then draw and cut a heart shape to fit the size of each cardboard square.

With an ice pick or scissors poke a small hole just to one side of the bottom of each heart.

Next, cut a 16-inch wire stem for each heart flower and slip the wire through the hole.

Now bend the wire and twist it together to form a stem.

To cover the wire, wrap green florist tape tightly around the stem.

Add interest with decorative rick-rack, braid or dainty lace.

Arrange the flowers and trim the flowerpot with a red velvet bow.

Valentine Favors

For special treats, make a small duplicate of your centerpiece, add one heart flower, and fill the pot with peppermint candies.

Rose-red Place Mats

Use red-and-white place mats to complement your Valentine table. Made from burlap, they're easy to care for, and quick to construct.

MATERIALS NEEDED:

red burlap—you will be able to get about 6 place mats from 1 yard of material
scissors
red thread
needle
yardstick
white felt

DIRECTIONS:

Cut the burlap into 12×18-inch rectangles. Follow one thread across the material when you cut, to get it perfectly straight.

Turn under a very tiny hem on the top and bottom of the place mat, and stitch this by hand or machine.

Make a 1-inch fringe on the two sides of the mat by pulling off the threads of material.

Then trace and cut small hearts from white felt, and sew them to the corners of each place mat.

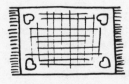

Heart-y Napkin Rings

Add a touch of heartfelt appeal with these pretty napkin rings.

MATERIALS NEEDED:

cardboard tube—from the middle of a waxed paper roll
knife with serrated edge
white glue
scissors
red velvet ribbon—1½ inches wide; approximately 7 inches for each napkin ring
2½-inch lightweight cardboard squares—1 for each napkin ring
2½-inch felt or fabric squares—1 for each napkin ring
rickrack, braid or lace (*optional*)

DIRECTIONS:

Measure and cut the cardboard tube into 1¼-inch rings. Use a knife with a serrated edge to make your work easier.

Spread glue on the outside of the cardboard ring and cover it with red velvet ribbon.

Next, glue a piece of felt to one side of each cardboard square, and let this dry.

Then draw and cut a heart shape from each square.

The hearts may be trimmed with rickrack, braid or lace, and then glued to the napkin rings.

Nosegay Candleholders

To complete your table and give it the look of an old-fashioned valentine card, set a romantic mood with these candleholders.

MATERIALS NEEDED:

clear glass candleholders
semigloss white enamel
paint brush
turpentine
small red and white plastic flowers
tall red candles

DIRECTIONS:

Paint the candleholders with white enamel and let them dry.

Then insert your candles, and fill the holder with tiny red and white flowers.

MAY DAY CENTERPIECE

Can you vaguely remember when—before the days of power politics—the first day of May heralded nothing more ominous than baskets of blossoms hung on doorknobs or perched on doorsteps?

Revive the age-old tradition of May merrymaking with this charming centerpiece. Starred with flowers and flaunting the softly shimmering tints of spring, it's as glad and as gay as the month it introduces!

MATERIALS NEEDED:

styrofoam disk—about 12 inches in diameter and 1 inch thick
empty cardboard tube—from the center of a roll of aluminum foil or waxed paper. It should be about 16 inches long.
green spray enamel
straight pins
scissors

satin ribbon—½ inch wide. You will need 1 yard each of 6 pastel colors.
white glue
1 large plastic flower—roughly 4 inches across the widest part; a pastel color.
artificial flowers—about 1 to 1½ inches across the widest part of the flower. A total of approximately 25 flowers will make a nice arrangement. Choose pastel colors to complement the ribbon.
wire cutters

DIRECTIONS:

The styrofoam disc will be used as a base for this arrangement.

Push the carboard tube firmly into the center of the styrofoam disk. Twist the tube a little as you push, to work it into the styrofoam.

Spread glue around the joint between the tube and the disk to be sure they'll stay together.

When the glue has set, spray the tube and disk with two coats of green paint, letting it dry completely after each application.

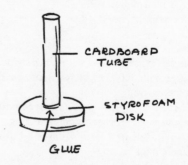

Arrange the small artificial flowers around the base of the cardboard tube, keeping the flowers within the circumference of the disk.

Use wire cutters to trim the stems when necessary, and then push the stems into the styrofoam to keep the flowers in place.

Use your imagination to create a tasteful arrangement, varying the lengths of the stems and the colors of the flowers.

One easy way to arrange the flowers is to make the stems of the flowers closest to the tube the longest, cutting the stems progressively shorter as you go out toward the edge of the disk. The result is delightful.

Next, make the streamers for the Maypole from satin ribbon.

Take one of the pastel ribbons you have selected and attach one end of it to the top of the Maypole.

To do this, fold about 1 inch of the ribbon inside the top of the cardboard tube and glue it down. It might be helpful to use a straight pin to hold the ribbon until the glue dries.

Then twist the ribbon halfway around the tube.

Attach the other end of the ribbon to the disc on the opposite side of the tube.

Trim off any excess ribbon, and fasten the end of the ribbon to the side of the styrofoam disk with a straight pin.

From the extra ribbon make a small bow to glue over the straight pin.

Continue making streamers, alternating the colors. Attach them one next to the other on the top of the pole, and spaced about 4 inches apart on the bottom, until there are streamers all around the Maypole.

As a finishing touch, cover the top of the cardboard tube with the large artificial flower.

Simply drop the stem into the tube, and the flower will hover gracefully over the Maypole.

FOURTH OF JULY CENTERPIECE

Red, white and blue are always fashionable, and never more so than on Independence Day!

Flag waving is never out of style, so get in the swing with this star-spangled centerpiece, blazing with the colors of Old Glory.

red, white and blue artificial flowers—enough to make an attractive arrangement on top of the drum. Choose approximately 3 large flowers of each color, and several smaller ones to use as fillers. Artificial carnations are a good size to work with, and usually come in all 3 colors.

blue hobby enamel—½ oz. bottle
small paint brush
turpentine

DIRECTIONS:

Paint the top and bottom rims of the drum with two coats of blue enamel, letting the paint dry thoroughly following each application.

When the paint is dry, cover the side of the drum between the top and bottom rims first with glue and then with red felt, which has been measured and cut to size.

MATERIALS NEEDED:

toy drum—an inexpensive metal one, at least 4 inches high and 7 inches in diameter

2 drumsticks—to go with the drum

red and white felt—1 10-inch square of each color

small American flag and flagpole—the flag should be about 4×6 inches

green styrofoam—a 3-inch cube is a good size. Look for styrofoam with an adhesive on one side.

florist clay—if your styrofoam does not come with an adhesive of some kind

4 yards red ribbon—1 inch wide; either plain satin ribbon or a lacy ribbon like that used for gift wrapping

wire cutters
white glue
straight pins
pencil
ruler

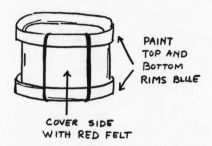

PAINT TOP AND BOTTOM RIMS BLUE

COVER SIDE WITH RED FELT

Draw and cut out eight stars from small squares of white felt.

Vary the size of the stars, keeping in mind that the large stars must stay within the size limitations of the red felt on the side of the drum.

Scatter the stars around the side of the drum, alternating the size for added interest, and attach them to the red felt with glue.

small flowers to fill any empty spaces between the larger ones.

Next, fasten the styrofoam block to the top of the drum.

If your styrofoam came with an adhesive on one side, simply press this onto the top of the drum. Otherwise, cover one side of the block with a thin layer of florist clay, and use this to hold the block in place.

Push the end of the flagpole into the center of the styrofoam block so the flag flies directly over the drum.

Finally, fill out the arrangement with five or six perky red bows. For full, fluffy bows, make one bow from five 2½-inch loops of ribbon.

To make one loop, take one 5-inch length of ribbon and fold it lightly in half.

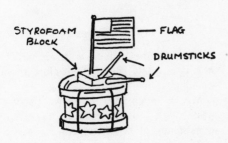

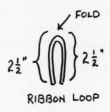

RIBBON LOOP

Then, using the diagram as a guide, attach the drumsticks by pushing the handles firmly into the styrofoam.

Add the red, white and blue flowers to the top of the drum in a pleasing arrangement.

Trim the stems of the flowers to about 3 or 4 inches in length, and then push the stems into the styrofoam.

Alternating the colors, cover the styrofoam block with flowers. Use the

Tie the five loops together at the bottom with string.

Then use a straight pin pushed through the bottom of the bow to attach it to the styrofoam.

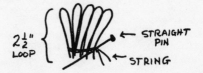

Place the bows in strategic locations, scattering them among the flowers.

Bows

HALLOWEEN PARTIES

These spirited Halloween decorations set the scene for mischief and mystery, and cause spooks and hobgoblins to shriek with glee. Even prowling witches will express their unqualified approval of your haunting decor!

Papier-mâché Pumpkin Centerpiece

Don't await the advent of the Great Pumpkin! Make a duplicate instead. His wide and gleaming grin will beckon young and old alike, and provide an eerie glow. Cunningly fashioned from papier-mâché, he looks almost like the real thing!

MATERIALS NEEDED:

1 large round balloon
wallpaper paste
newspaper
orange semigloss enamel
paint brush
turpentine
orange and green yarn—1 small skein
    of each
black felt—one 10-inch square
white glue
scissors

DIRECTIONS:

First, fill the balloon with air until it is completely round; then close the opening at the top.

Mix a small amount of wallpaper paste with water, until it has the consistency of thick soup.

Tear the newspaper into approximately 1-inch squares, and soak in paste.

Cover the balloon with three or four layers of paste-soaked squares, smoothing each square carefully as you work. Be sure the balloon is entirely covered with newspaper squares, as any uncovered space can result in a gaping hole when the papier-mâché dries.

To make a stem for the pumpkin, wrap several strips of newspaper soaked in paste around the top of the balloon.

Put the covered balloon up on an empty tin can for 24 hours, or until the papier-mâché is completely dry.

Then paint the papier-mâché with orange enamel. Let this dry, and apply a second coat if necessary.

When this is dry, use orange yarn to form the lines of the pumpkin, gluing them in place.

Wind and glue green yarn around the stem until it's completely covered.

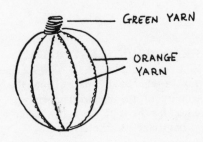

The Face: Cut eyes, nose and mouth from black felt, and glue them in their proper positions.

Now promote the pumpkin to the place of honor on your table, and surround him with fruit, nuts and fall leaves.

Jack-o'-Lantern Favors

Tiny white-sheeted ghosts and trick-or-treat pranksters will be entranced with a jack-o'-lantern of their very own. Filled with candies, nuts and fruit, jack-o'-lanterns make perfect favors. Or you might scatter them around your home within easy reach of eager fingers.

DIRECTIONS:

Using smaller balloons, cover them in the same manner as your centerpiece.

When the papier-mâché has dried, use a knife to cut off the top of each pumpkin.

Then paint and decorate the favors in the same fashion as the centerpiece.

Tempting Tablecloth

Cast a spell over all your guests with this sorcerer's tablecloth.

MATERIALS NEEDED:

1 inexpensive light orange or white sheet or tablecloth
felt cloth squares of orange, black and green
white glue
orange yarn—1 small skein
scissors
orange thread—1 spool
needle

DIRECTIONS:

Cut ten or more 4-inch circles of orange felt.

From green felt, cut a 1-inch stem for each circle. Glue the stems to the circles.

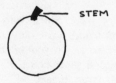

Glue orange yarn on each felt circle to form the lines of a pumpkin.

Make the eyes, nose and mouth of each jack-o'-lantern from black felt, holding each piece in place with glue.

Using tiny stitches, sew the felt pumpkins to the sheet or tablecloth with orange thread.

Black Magic Candleholders

The dimly flickering light of candles can add a touch of witchcraft. These candleholders will materialize in a matter of seconds!

MATERIALS NEEDED:

clear glass candleholders
semigloss black enamel
paint brush
turpentine
tall orange candles
nuts or Halloween candies (*optional*)

DIRECTIONS:

Paint the candleholders with black enamel; let them dry, and insert your candles.

Then fill the holders with nuts or candies.

GRADUATION CENTERPIECE

For a change of pace from the solemnity of the commencement exercises, it's hard to beat this beaming, bespectacled scholar.

Glowing with youthful exuberance and smugly self-assured, he's the personification of graduates everywhere!

MATERIALS NEEDED:

white styrofoam ball—about 2½ inches in diameter
1 yard white nylon net
scissors
ruler
white string
12 inches thick yarn—any color but black
black felt—1 5-inch square
white glue
red felt—1 small circle the size of a quarter
white felt—about 8 square inches
black poster board or cardboard
straight pins
cardboard tube—about 8 inches long; from the center of a waxed paper or aluminum foil roll
black spray paint—gloss, semigloss or flat
styrofoam disk—about 6 inches in diameter and 1½ inches thick

DIRECTIONS:

Begin by spraying the styrofoam disk with two coats of black paint, letting the paint dry after each application.

Then cover the cardboard tube with glue and a piece of white felt, which has been measured and cut to fit.

When the glue has set, push the felt-covered tube into the center of one side of the styrofoam disk. Push them firmly together, and spread glue around the point where the tube and the disk meet to ensure their strength.

Attach the other end of the felt-covered tube to the styrofoam ball in the same manner, pushing it into the ball and applying glue to the joint.

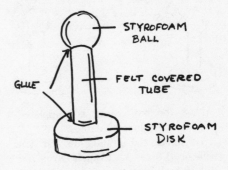

Next, cut the whole yard of white net into 6-inch squares. Do this as carefully as possible, but don't worry if each square is not perfect.

Working with one net square at a time, tie a piece of string around the middle of the square, pull it tight and tie a knot.

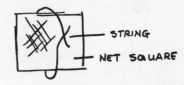

Trim off any excess string, and push a straight pin through the center of the net square. Then push the pin firmly into the styrofoam ball.

Continue adding net squares, one next to the other, until the styrofoam ball is completely covered, and you have what looks like a big net ball.

Then take the yarn and shove 1 inch of it through the hole to the inside of the hat. Attach this to the inside of the hat with glue.

Tie a knot 2 inches from the other end of the yarn, and fluff out the end strands to make a tassel.

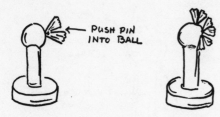

PUSH PIN INTO BALL

Now the basic head is completed, and it's time to add details.

To make the graduation hat you will need one 3×15-inch strip and one 8-inch square of black poster board.

Make a ring from the 3×15-inch strip of poster board. Bend and glue the ends together at the back of the ring.

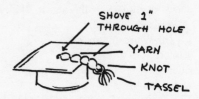

SHOVE 1" THROUGH HOLE

YARN

KNOT

TASSEL

Draw and cut a large pair of glasses from a 16×4-inch piece of black poster board, bending the bows of the glasses to make them look realistic.

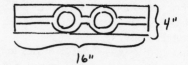

4"

16"

GLUE 2 ENDS TOGETHER

Glue the 8-inch square on top of the ring, making sure the ring is centered in the middle of the square.

BEND BOWS

Perch the graduation cap on top of the head, and add the glasses in the appropriate spot.

Several straight pins poked through the bows of the glasses into the net will hold them in place.

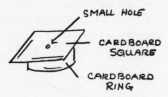

SMALL HOLE

CARDBOARD SQUARE

CARDBOARD RING

Make a small hole in the center of the square with the point of a scissors.

STRAIGHT PIN

Cut out two eyes and a mouth from black felt, and a round, quarter-sized nose from red felt. Attach these to the head with a little glue.

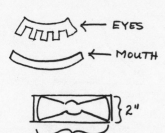

EYES

MOUTH

2"

6"

Finally, make a bow tie from a 2 × 6-inch piece of poster board and glue it to the neck of the graduate.

LITTLE PARTIES

Important holidays and special occasions provide us with reasons and ideas for parties and decoration. But the most popular—and frequent—form of entertainment are those little informal affairs, usually given for no other reason than to share a few hours of fun and small talk with congenial friends.

Since these little parties are so big in entertainment value, why not decorate for them, too? You'll find the results tremendously rewarding!

Exotic Foreign Cuisine

An excursion into the realms of foreign cookery can be a delightful adventure and adds zest and glamour to everyday menus.

When featuring one or more foreign dishes, enhance the international flavor of your meal with this unusual centerpiece, flying the flags of the countries represented.

This particular project may require a bit of research with a handy world almanac, encyclopedia or in the nearest public library, but it's well worth the effort, for, in addition to dressing up your table, it provides a unique conversation piece.

MATERIALS NEEDED:

1 piece of rock—to be used as the base or "island" of the centerpiece. A piece of lava, coral or quartz is perfect, but any rock can be

used. If you prefer, you can make your own island from children's modeling clay. It should be roughly 6 inches long and wide, and 5 inches high.

florist clay

5 black wire coat hangers

wire cutters

5 pieces of cardboard—3 × 5 inches; poster board is fine

white glue

ruler

scissors

pencil

10 artificial flowers—each about 1½ inches across the widest part, in colors to complement the flags. Use paper, plastic, cloth or velvet flowers.

masking tape

felt or construction paper—the colors found in the flags you have decided to make. To make 5 flags, you will need 5 10½ × 3-inch pieces of felt or construction paper. These will be used for the background of each flag. You will need additional material or paper to add the appropriate designs or emblems to the flags.

DIRECTIONS:

First you must decide which flags you intend to make. You might use the flag from just one country, or flags from several different ones.

Look up the flag or flags in a research book. This will tell you what color should be used as the background for the flag and the emblem or emblems on it. It might be a good idea to keep the book within easy reach for quick reference while you work.

Use wire cutters to cut one flagpole from each of the five wire coat hangers.

Cutting them from the straight side of the hangers, make two 10-inch flagpoles, two 12-inch flagpoles, and one 13-inch flagpole.

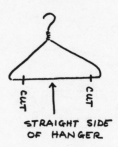

STRAIGHT SIDE OF HANGER

Attach a 3 × 5-inch cardboard rectangle to one end of a wire flagpole with three pieces of masking tape.

Place the tape on one side of the cardboard, pull it tight around the wire and fasten it to the other side of the cardboard. Connect the cardboard to the wire in three different places.

Tape one piece of cardboard to each flagpole in this manner.

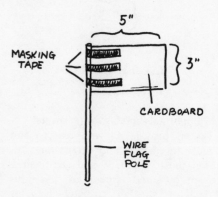

From construction paper or felt, cut a 10½ × 3-inch rectangle for each flag in the correct background color.

Cover one flag at a time.

First, fold one piece of felt or

construction paper in half. Place this fold over the wire on the flagpole so the two halves of the felt cover both sides of the cardboard. Use glue, spread evenly on both sides of the cardboard, to attach the felt or construction paper.

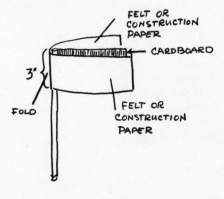

To add stripes, bars, crosses, stars, etc., to the flag, cut the emblems from felt or construction paper, and glue them to the proper spot.

Use a small ball of florist clay to attach each flagpole to your rock "island."

Press the clay firmly onto the rock and then push the flagpole into it. If you made your own rock out of modeling clay, you won't need the florist clay. Simply push the end of the flagpole into the clay.

Arrange the flags so they fly over the island at jaunty angles. Then place the artificial flowers at the base of the flagpoles to hide the florist clay.

Trim the stems of the flowers to about 1 inch in length, and then push the stems into the florist clay.

By the way, you might use empty wine bottles as candleholders to heighten the continental atmosphere.

Spring Flower Ball

Give your table the look of a magic garden with this luminous centerpiece of bright spring flowers.

Warm and alive with color, it's as dazzling as a handful of sunshine.

MATERIALS NEEDED:

styrofoam ball—about 3 inches in
diameter is a good size

small plastic flowers—about 40 flowers with the leaves should be
enough. These usually come in a
bunch of 5 or 6 flowers to one
stem. Any color will do, because
you'll be painting the flowers any-
way.

½ inch wood doweling—14 inches
long

flowerpot

styrofoam—to fit inside the flowerpot

green velvet ribbon—½ inch wide
and 1 yard long

green felt—enough to cover the top
of the flowerpot

scissors

gloss spray enamel—two or three
different colors of your choice.
Yellow, red and orange or blue,
green and white make attractive
combinations.

green hobby enamel—¼ oz. bottle

paint brush

turpentine

white glue

straight pins

wire cutters

DIRECTIONS:

Cut the stem of each flower so
only a 1½-inch stem remains. Also
cut the stems on the leaves to 1½
inches.

Divide the flowers and leaves into
two or three equal groups, one group
for each color paint you have selected.

Spray the flowers and leaves in
the first group with one enamel,
and paint the second group with
enamel of another color. If you are
using three colors, paint the last
group with the third color.

Paint both sides of each flower
three times, letting the paint dry
after each application. This will give
the flowers the appearance of cloi-
sonné.

Next, paint the wood doweling
with green hobby enamel. Let it dry,
give it a second coat, and dry again.

Place the styrofoam inside the
flowerpot. Then measure and cut a
piece of felt to fit on the top of the
flowerpot to cover the styrofoam.

Make a small hole, ½ inch in
diameter, in the center of the felt
circle, and place the felt on top of
the styrofoam.

Push one end of the dowel
through the hole into the styrofoam.
The dowel should now be sticking
straight up in the air.

Then take the styrofoam ball and
push it onto the other end of the
dowel.

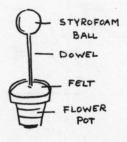

The idea is to cover the entire ball with the painted flowers and leaves.

To do this, dip the end of each flower stem in glue, and push it into the styrofoam ball. Continue adding blossoms as closely together as possible until the entire ball is covered.

To add a smart velvet bow to the flower ball, cut the ribbon into two equal pieces. Tie each into a bow, and lay one atop the other.

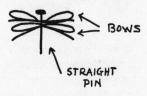

Put a pin through the center of both bows, and stick the pin into the bottom of the styrofoam ball close to the dowel.

Fall Basket

The warm browns and tawny richness of nuts and pine cones gleam through the barest touch of autum-

nal color to make this vibrant fall arrangement a distinctive and dramatic centerpiece.

MATERIALS NEEDED:

round straw basket—at least 5 inches in diameter and 2 or 3 inches high. Natural straw is the most suitable color.
styrofoam ball—to fill the basket
florist clay
3 yards velvet ribbon—¼ inch wide; the same color as the paint you select, or an accent color
gloss spray enamel—in a color of your choice
scissors
straight pins
flexible wire
wire cutters
small drill
white glue
string
newspaper
assorted nuts in the shell—walnuts, pecans, almonds, hazelnuts
small pine cones

DIRECTIONS:

Begin by covering the bottom of the inside of the basket with a layer of florist clay, and push the styrofoam ball into the clay. This will keep the ball firmly in place.

That portion of the styrofoam ball that sticks up above the basket should be covered completely with nuts and pine cones.

To do this, a short wire stem must be connected to each nut and pine cone.

First, drill a small hole in the end or side of each nut.

Then cut a 2-inch piece of wire, dip one end of the wire in glue, and insert it into the hole. Make a stem for each nut in this manner.

Fasten a wire stem to each pine cone by wrapping a piece of wire around the bottom of the cone.

Attach the nuts and pine cones to the styrofoam ball by dipping each stem in glue and pushing the stems into the styrofoam. Intermix the various types of nuts with the pine cones, and place them as closely together as possible.

After the glue has set, wrap several layers of newspaper around the basket, but do not cover the nuts and pine cones. This will protect the basket while you spray paint the arrangement.

When you have covered the basket, spray the nuts and pine cones with the enamel you have chosen.

Hold the can about 12 inches from the centerpiece and paint quickly, so just a light coat of color covers the nuts and cones, and some of the original browns show through.

Let the paint dry, remove the newspaper, and add crisp velvet bows to complete the centerpiece.

Make each bow from three loops of ribbon.

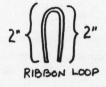

RIBBON LOOP

To form one loop, take a 4-inch piece of ribbon and fold it lightly in half. Make three of these loops and tie them together at the bottom with string.

Use a straight pin pushed through the bottom of the bow to fasten it to the styrofoam.

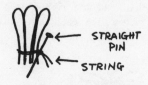

STRAIGHT PIN

STRING

You should get nine bows from the 3 yards of ribbon. Sprinkle these at random throughout the arrangement between the nuts and pine cones.

BOWS

Summer Flowers

Real flowers may wilt and die beneath the blistering kiss of the summer sun, but these airy tissue-paper blossoms never lose their cool.

Try them—they're as tart and as refreshing as a tall drink!

MATERIALS NEEDED:

tissue paper—1 or 2 sheets of 2 or 3 colors of your choice
green tissue paper—2 sheets

flexible wire
florist tape
staples and stapler
scissors
ruler
pencil

Crush the folded end of the roll tightly together and secure it with a staple.

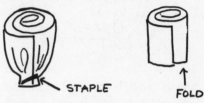

Then fringe the top of the roll into approximately ¼-inch strips.

DIRECTIONS:

Although some tissue-paper flowers are difficult and time-consuming to construct, these are specifically designed to take very little effort and even less time.

The directions can easily be altered to make bigger or smaller flowers by using larger or smaller pieces of paper.

Begin by making the center of one flower. Cut a 7×12-inch rectangle from tissue paper (any color but green).

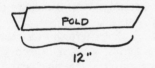

Fold the paper in half lengthwise and roll it up loosely.

To make the outer petals of the flower, cut a 7×30-inch rectangle from tissue paper of a contrasting color, and fold it in half lengthwise.

Roll this strip of paper loosely around the fringed flower center. Place it so the fold is at the bottom of the flower.

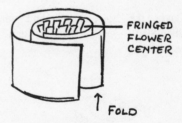

Crush the bottom of this roll together too, and fasten it with a staple.

Be sure to staple through both the bottom of the outer petals and the bottom of the flower center.

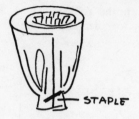

— STAPLE

Form leaves for the flowers by cutting six 1½ ×3-inch rectangles from green tissue paper.

Lay each piece of paper squarely on top of one another and hold them all together at one of the narrow ends. This end will become the bottom of the leaves.

Then use scissors to trim the other end of the rectangle to a point.

Gently fold, bend and turn the upper edges of the flower outward to make the petals look more realistic.

Make a hole in the bottom of the flower, pull a wire through the hole and twist it together to form a stem.

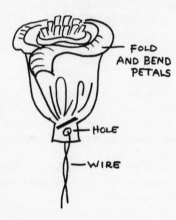

FOLD AND BEND PETALS

HOLE

WIRE

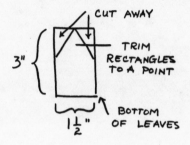

CUT AWAY

TRIM RECTANGLES TO A POINT

3"

BOTTOM OF LEAVES

1½"

Crush the bottom of the leaves together and fasten it with a staple.

Cover the hole, staple and wire with florist tape wound tightly around it.

STAPLE

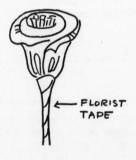

FLORIST TAPE

Fan out the tops of the six leaves by separating and bending them gently.

Poke a hole through the bottom of the leaves, pull an 8-inch piece of wire through the hole and twist it together. Wind florist tape around the bottom of the leaves and the wire stem.

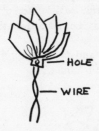

Finally, attach the leaves to the flowers by winding tape around the leaf and flower stems.

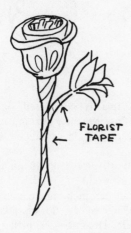

When you've completed your centerpiece, try making miniature flowers, using toothpicks as stems. Then, just for fun, place one on top of each baked potato, piece of meat or slice of pie. This is a quick and easy way to add spice to any meal.

Pop Art Flowers

There's one thing about pop art—nobody's neutral on the subject!

Whether you're pro or con, you'll be fascinated by these sturdy and fanciful flowers. Use them anywhere, any time—but they're most appro-priate in the patio or on a sun deck. In wild and wonderful color combinations, they're strictly a la mode!

MATERIALS NEEDED:

empty tin cans—cans made of very lightweight tin are the best because they are so easy to cut
tin cutters
flexible wire
ice pick
hammer
small scrap of wood
gloss spray enamel—2 or 3 harmonious colors
hobby enamel—2 or 3 different colors to contrast with the colors of the spray enamel
paint brush
turpentine
pencil
florist tape
can opener
vase with a narrow neck or an empty bottle of an unusual shape

DIRECTIONS:

The size of each flower will vary, depending upon the size of each tin can. This variety in size will make the final arrangement more attractive, as large and small flowers will be used.

Follow the same basic directions for all of the flowers, but alter the dimensions according to the size of the tin can.

Make the largest flowers about 4 inches in diameter, and the smallest 2 inches in diameter.

To make one flower, use a can opener to remove the bottom and top from a tin can. Cut the side of the can open with tin cutters. Then flatten out the can, and remove any paper or labels.

↑ CUT SIDE OF CAN OPEN

Draw and cut one small circle and one large circle from the tin. The small circle should be approximately two thirds the size of the larger one. It's not necessary to be exact, as a little difference one way or the other won't matter.

The flower center will be made from the small circle.

With tin cutters, make a cut from the edge of the small circle in toward the middle of the circle. Stop about ½ inch from the middle of the circle. DO NOT CUT ALL THE WAY TO THE MIDDLE.

MIDDLE OF CIRCLE

Continue making cuts every ¼ inch until you have gone all the way around the circle.

Here are two different patterns which may be used for the flower petals.

Enlarge and cut one of them from the large tin circle.

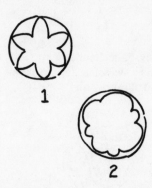

1

2

When this is completed, lay the fringed flower center on top of the petals, centering it as much as possible.

Place both pieces of tin on top of a scrap of wood.

With an ice pick, make two holes in the center of the flower, about ½ inch apart. Hold the ice pick in position, and then tap the handle with a hammer until it makes a hole in both layers of tin. *Don't forget the scrap of wood*—it will keep the ice pick from going into your table top.

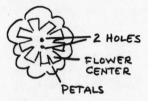

2 HOLES

FLOWER CENTER

PETALS

To construct a stem, take a 24-inch piece of wire and fold it in half. Then push it through the two

holes in the top of the flower, and
twist it tightly together.

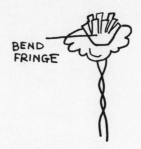

BEND
FRINGE

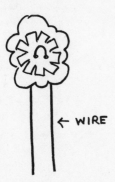

← WIRE

A dozen flowers, some of each
style, would be a good number to
fill an average-sized vase or bottle.

When you have completed as
many flowers as you wish to make,
divide them into two or three
groups, one group for each color
spray enamel you have selected.

Paint each flower with three coats
of enamel, letting the paint dry thoroughly after each application.

The easiest way to do this is to
place the stems of all the flowers
you want in one color in an empty
bottle. Then you can spray paint
both sides of each flower at the
same time.

Next, bend the fringe on the flower
center up to make it three-dimensional, and to hide the holes and
wire in the middle of the flower.

If you used pattern #1, bend and
curve the petals up slightly.

After the paint has dried, use
hobby enamel to decorate the petals
of each flower with scallops, stripes,
zigzags, polka dots or creative designs.

You can also paint the fringed
flower centers to contrast with the
petals. Let your imagination go, have
fun and make each a fanciful and
unique "work of art."

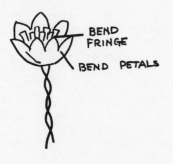

BEND
FRINGE

BEND PETALS

Decorate all the flowers, let them
dry, and finish by wrapping green
florist tape tightly around each stem.

For pattern #2, leave the petals
flat.

Seasonal and Holiday Decorations

Every season of the year offers us an opportunity to make our homes come alive. In this chapter you will find decorations designed to provide your home with a season ticket to fun and frolic, and to welcome each new season with a clash of cymbals.

And since most of us reserve our major decorating efforts for the Yuletide season, you'll find a number of original and imaginative ideas to greet Father Christmas with a lift of laughter and a wealth of color.

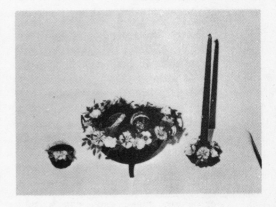

THE EASTER PARADE

Easter—when children eagerly await the coming of that world-famous rabbit, and the pipes of Pan assault the ears of winter-weary adults with their lilting melody.

Use this Easter finery to make your home a candidate "for the rotogravure" and scent it with the flowering breath of spring.

Springtime-Fresh Centerpiece

For a deliciously different Easter basket, try this sparkling centerpiece.

Foaming with net and garlanded by flowers, it's as young as springtime!

MATERIALS NEEDED:

1 metal colander
flat or semigloss spray enamel—any color
5 or 6 styrofoam eggs
brass sequin pins
sequins—an assortment of delicate colors
½ yard green net

20 small plastic flowers—pastel colors to complement the color of the sequins

½ pint gloss or semigloss varnish

½ pint turpentine

½ small bottle of gold paint

DIRECTIONS:

Paint the colander with spray enamel. Let this dry, and apply another coat.

When the second coat of paint has dried, line the colander with green net, folding and fluffing the net to make it fit.

Next, cover the styrofoam eggs with pastel-colored sequins. Put a pin through the middle of each sequin, and push the pins into the styrofoam.

Use your imagination to form color patterns or stripes with sequins, or simply make each egg a solid color.

Then fill the colander with sequined eggs, arranged atop the nest of net.

To make the antiquing mixture for the plastic flowers, mix in an empty coffee can ½ pint gloss or semigloss varnish with ½ pint turpentine and ½ small bottle of gold paint.

Dip the flowers into the antiquing mixture, swishing them on the bottom of the can to pick up gold paint on the petals. Then hang the flowers upside down on a clothesline to dry. Shake the line occasionally to prevent the accumulation of excess paint.

Finally, when the flowers are dry, encircle the rim of the colander with the small antiqued flowers.

Fun 'n' Flower Favors

These lively trifles will tickle the fancy of all youngsters from seven to seventy. Fill them with candles, place them in strategic nooks and crannies, and stand back to watch the fun!

MATERIALS NEEDED:

small individual metal molds used for gelatin desserts and salads

flat or semigloss spray enamel—any color. You may use the same paint as was used on the colander.

green net—a 6-inch square for each mold

small plastic flowers—one for each favor. They should match those used for the centerpiece.

DIRECTIONS:

Spray paint each mold with enamel. When the paint is dry, apply a second coat and let it dry again.

Line each mold with gauzy green net, add an antiqued flower to one side of the nest, and fill with candy Easter eggs.

Flowery Candleholders

Flower-filled candleholders are as refreshing as spring rain.

MATERIALS NEEDED:

clear glass candleholders

semigloss spray enamel—the same color used to paint the colander centerpiece

small plastic flowers—to match those used in the centerpiece. Use 5 or 6 flowers for each holder.

candles—any pastel color

DIRECTIONS:

Spray the candleholders with enamel, let them dry, and apply another coat.

When the paint has dried, add your candles and fill the holders with antiqued flowers.

Easter Egg Napkin Rings

As a final flourish, match your centerpiece with these sparkly napkin rings. Children will love them!

MATERIALS NEEDED:

cardboard tube—from the middle of a waxed paper roll

knife with serrated edge

white glue

scissors

ruler

2½-inch lightweight cardboard squares—1 for each napkin ring

2½-inch squares of white felt—1 for each napkin ring

sequins—Easter egg colors

pastel-colored velvet ribbon—1½ inches wide and 7 inches long for each napkin ring

DIRECTIONS:

Measure and cut the cardboard tube into 1¼-inch rings, using a knife with a serrated edge.

Then cover each cardboard ring with glue and a 7-inch strip of velvet ribbon.

Spread glue on one side of each cardboard square, and cover with a square of white felt.

Cut an egg shape from each covered square and decorate it with sequins. Arrange the sequins in interesting color patterns or candy-cane stripes, and glue them to the felt.

Finally, glue one glittering egg to the top of each napkin ring.

THANKSGIVING (DRESS UP YOUR HOME)

Golden-brown turkey and tangy cranberry sauce, flaky pumpkin and mince pies, steaming mounds of mouth-watering vegetables, luscious jams and jellies, crisp salad, and honey-sweet fruit adorn your table and tempt the taste buds.

Make your Thanksgiving feast a treat for the eye as well as the palate with these brilliant decorations, designed in the autumn colors.

Horn of Plenty Centerpiece

A horn of plenty is a traditional Thanksgiving accessory, signifying the abundant gifts of a bountiful land. For a traditional decoration done in a delightfully untraditional manner, try this one.

MATERIALS NEEDED:

1 foot of chicken wire

flat or semigloss spray enamel—any color may be used. Black is particularly effective because it gives the wire the appearance of wrought iron.

velvet ribbon—¼ or ¾ inch wide; 1 foot each of 3 or 4 different fall colors

wire cutters

an assortment of nuts—walnuts, pecans, almonds, etc. Use those which are still in the shell.

Treasure Gold Wax Gilt

½ yard green net

DIRECTIONS:

To bend, roll and twist the chicken wire into the shape of a cornucopia or a horn of plenty:

First roll the wire to make what looks like a large ice-cream cone.

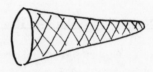

Then gently bend the tip of the cone up a little bit.

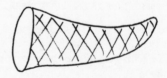

Chicken wire is very flexible and easy to manipulate, so don't be afraid to try it. If your first attempt doesn't look just right, try again.

Spray the cornucopia with two coats of enamel, letting the paint dry thoroughly between coats.

After the second coat has dried, make colorful stripes around the cornucopia by weaving ribbon in and out of the chicken wire.

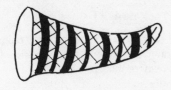

Attach both ends of each piece of ribbon to the bottom of the horn with white glue.

Line the inside of the horn with green net by folding and shaping the net until it fits neatly.

Finally, fill the cornucopia to over-flowing with papier-mâché fruit and gilded nuts. (To gild the nuts, simply rub Treasure Gold on each nut with your fingers, and polish with a clean cloth until lustrous.)

Papier-mâché Fruit

This colorful papier-mâché fruit is especially designed to enhance the appeal of your horn of plenty.

MATERIALS NEEDED:

inexpensive plastic fruit
wallpaper paste
newspaper
heavy string
flat or semigloss enamel—a variety
  of colors to paint the fruit
black or brown enamel—for antiquing
paint brush
turpentine
clear varnish

DIRECTIONS:

Stir water and wallpaper paste to-gether. Tear the newspaper into 1½-inch squares and soak in paste. Paste these squares onto the fruit until all the plastic is completely covered. For small areas which are hard to cover, use even smaller squares of newspaper.

Arrange paste-soaked string on the fruit to make interesting line designs.

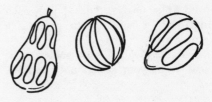

Let the papier-mâché dry thor-oughly and paint the fruit. Each piece may be painted one solid color or a number of colors.

When the enamel has dried, an-tique the fruit by brushing over it very lightly with black or brown paint. This will accent the string de-signs by adding shadows and high-lights to the fruit.

Give the fruit a finishing coat of varnish, and let dry.

Nut-filled Candleholders

Use these graceful candleholders to accentuate the image of peaceful prosperity.

MATERIALS NEEDED:

clear glass candleholders
spray enamel—the same color used
  to paint the centerpiece

an assortment of nuts in the shell
Treasure Gold Wax Gilt
candles—any color to harmonize
with the colors used in the centerpiece

DIRECTIONS:

Spray the candleholders with enamel and let the paint dry. Then
apply a second coat and dry again.

While the paint is drying, gild nuts
by rubbing Treasure Gold on them
with your fingers. Then polish each
nut with a soft rag to produce a
soft glow.

Fill the holders with golden nuts,
and insert your selection of candles.

Fruitful Tablecloth

Provide the good gobbler with a
fitting background by using a tablecloth festooned with felt fruit ap-

pliqués in the colors of autumn
leaves.

MATERIALS NEEDED:

felt—a variety of fruit colors:
    orange, yellow, red, green, and
    brown or black
scissors
white glue
yarn—2 or 3 colors which comple-
    ment your felt
tablecloth—a color to set off your
    table decorations
needle
thread
snaps (*optional*)

DIRECTIONS:

Cut realistic, life-sized fruit shapes
from vivid felt.

To trim a complete tablecloth,
you will need about four pieces of
each type of fruit; for example, four
apples, four oranges, four pears.

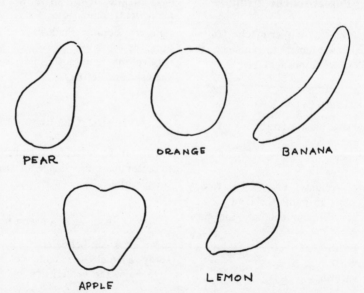

PEAR   ORANGE   BANANA

APPLE   LEMON

Cut small black or brown felt stems, and glue one to the top of each apple and pear.

Then decorate each piece of fruit with fanciful line designs by gluing bright yarn to the felt.

Be sure to make the yarn patterns match the string designs on the papier-mâché fruit in your centerpiece.

Scatter the felt fruit around the bottom of your tablecloth, and sew each piece securely in place.

If you prefer, you may sew a snap to the back of each piece of fruit and to the tablecloth so the decorations can be easily changed for various festive occasions.

Colorful Napkin Rings

Your guests will be enthralled with these pretty napkin rings, spangled with sun-ripened fruit.

MATERIALS NEEDED:

cardboard tube—from the middle of a waxed paper roll
white glue
yarn—several accent colors
velvet ribbon—1½ inches wide; 1 7-inch strip for each napkin ring. Use a variety of fall colors.
scissors
felt—various fruit colors, such as red, orange, yellow, green and brown or black
knife with serrated edge
ruler

DIRECTIONS:

Measure and cut 1¼-inch rings from the cardboard tube, using a knife with a serrated edge.

Spread glue on the outside of each cardboard ring, and cover with velvet ribbon.

From 2½-inch felt squares, cut small fruit shapes. You will need one piece of fruit for each napkin ring.

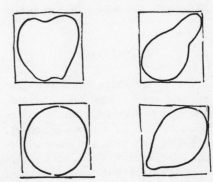

Attach a small brown or black felt stem to each apple and pear with glue.

Now glue yarn on each piece of fruit to form simple line designs. The designs should match those on the papier-mâché fruit used in the centerpiece.

Then fasten one miniature fruit to each napkin ring with glue.

CHRISTMAS

Deck you home with boughs of holly and everything gay, glittering and glamorous! These spectacular Christmas decorations are easy to make, and creating them is sheer delight. And remember—it's never too early to begin getting ready!

Nut Tree

The glossy sheen of this elegant nut tree catches and holds the mellow light of Christmas candles. Generally used as a Christmas accessory, it blends well with any seasonal decor. (Incidentally, if you've a generous source of nuts and a heaping helping of patience, this is a lasting and thoughtful gift for favorite friends and relatives.)

MATERIALS NEEDED:

styrofoam cone—at least 12 inches tall

assortment of nuts in the shell, such as walnuts, pecans, brazil nuts and almonds

flexible wire

wire cutters
small drill
white glue
tree stand—an inverted glass, bowl or vase may be used
green or red velvet ribbon—1 inch wide, ½ yard long
clear gloss varnish
paint brush
turpentine

DIRECTIONS:

The idea is to cover the entire styrofoam cone with an assortment of nuts.

To do this, you must first drill a small hole in the end or side of each nut.

Next, cut a 2-inch wire stem; dip one end of the wire in glue and insert it into the hole. Make a stem for each nut in this manner.

To attach the nuts to the tree, dip each stem in glue and push the stems into the styrofoam.

It's easier to start at the bottom of the cone and work your way up until the cone is completely covered with nuts.

When you have finished attaching the nuts, let the glue set until the nuts are fixed securely in place.

Then paint the tree with clear gloss varnish. Be sure to coat each nut thoroughly with the varnish to bring out the rich brown tones in the shells.

Place the tree on a stand made from an inverted glass, bowl or vase, and use a velvet bow at the base of the tree to provide a merry splash of color.

Christmas Centerpiece

This gleaming centerpiece has the impact of a burst of trumpets. Burnished gold leaves swirl about a jeweled candle to kindle a halo of light and sparkling color.

MATERIALS NEEDED:

styrofoam ring—at least 12 inches in diameter

metallic gold spray paint
flexible wire
wire cutters
white glue
ice pick
1 large candle—a candle in a glittering glass container is ideal
an assortment of dried leaves, pine cones, nuts, holly, berries, seeds; even artificial flowers may be used

DIRECTIONS:

First, cover the top of the styrofoam ring with dried leaves of various sizes and shapes. To do this, dip the stem of each leaf in glue and push the stems firmly into the styrofoam.

Position the leaves so the stems are attached near the opening in the middle of the ring.

OPENING IN
MIDDLE OF RING

TOP VIEW

Fill out the arrangement with a generous amount of pine cones, nuts, dried berries, seeds or artificial flowers. Place these objects between and on top of the leaves.

You will have to attach a short piece of wire to any object which does not have a stem. Use an ice pick to pierce a hole, insert the wire, and bend or twist it slightly to keep it in place.

Be sure to dip each stem or piece of wire in glue before pushing it into the styrofoam.

When the arrangement is complete, spray it with gold paint and let it dry.

It may require a number of coats to cover all of the objects with gold. Remember to let each coat dry before applying the next one.

Any styrofoam which shows through should also be sprayed gold to make it blend inconspicuously into the arrangement.

After the last coat of paint has dried, place a large glittery candle in the center of the ring.

These same directions may also be used to make a golden wreath. Simply omit the candle and attach a small wire loop to the back of the styrofoam ring to hang the wreath.

Antiqued Christmas Tree

Let your door or your wall bloom with roses in December. Feathery light and flecked with gold, this fairytale tree of scarlet roses and velvety green foliage is an enchanting bit of Yuletide foolery.

tree, the two long sides of the triangle should be about 22 inches and the short side about 16 inches. However, this may be made smaller or larger if you prefer.

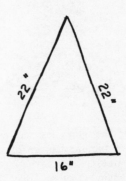

Paint one side of the cardboard triangle with green enamel and let it dry.

In the meantime, antique the artificial leaves and roses. To do this, mix ½ pint glossy clear varnish with an equal amount of turpentine. Add ½ bottle of gold paint, and stir thoroughly. Then dip each leaf and flower into this antiquing mixture.

Use clothespins to hang the leaves and flowers upside down on a clothesline to dry. Shake the clothesline occasionally while they are drying. This will prevent the accumulation of excess paint on the petals.

When the cardboard triangle, leaves and roses are dry, the tree may be assembled.

First, cover the painted side of the triangle with green leaves. Remove each leaf from its stem and attach it to the cardboard with a large drop of glue.

Glue the red roses among the leaves to form a becoming pattern,

MATERIALS NEEDED:

very heavy cardboard—1 side of a large cardboard box may be used
scissors
white glue
flat or semigloss green enamel
paint brush
½ pint glossy clear varnish
turpentine
1 small bottle of gold paint
plastic green leaves—an assortment of different sizes and shapes
8–10 large artificial red roses
red velvet ribbon—1½ inches wide, 1 yard long
1 adhesive picture hanger

DIRECTIONS:

Make the foundation of your tree by cutting a large triangle from heavy cardboard. For a good-sized

and add a bold red velvet bow to the bottom of the tree with a little glue.

After the glue has set, attach an adhesive picture hanger to the back of the tree.

The same method may be used to cover a large cardboard ring with leaves and flowers to make an antiqued wreath.

Christmas Tree Ornaments

These imaginative tree ornaments will give your tree the magical shimmer of the northern lights.

Use them to array your Christmas tree with cascades of color, the brightness of stars, the subtle glint of spun gold, or strew it with flowers.

Antiqued Flower Ball

MATERIALS NEEDED:

styrofoam ball
tiny plastic flowers—enough to cover the ball completely
wire cutters
4-inch piece of flexible wire
velvet ribbon—¼ inch wide; 10 inches of a color to complement the flowers
white glue
½ pint gloss varnish
½ pint turpentine
½ bottle gold paint

DIRECTIONS:

Mix the ½ pint gloss varnish, the ½ pint turpentine and the ½ bot-

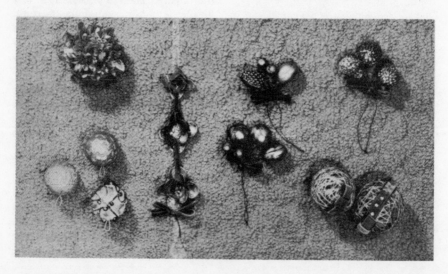

tle of gold paint in an empty coffee can and stir vigorously.

Hold each flower by the stem and dip it into the antiquing solution, swishing it on the bottom of the can to pick up the gold paint.

Hang the flowers upside down on a clothesline to dry. Shake the line once in a while to remove any excess paint from the petals.

When the paint has dried, cut the stem of each flower so only a 1-inch piece of stem remains

Dip the end of each flower stem in glue and push it into the styrofoam ball.

Place the flowers as closely together as possible, and continue adding blossoms until the entire ball is covered.

Next, make a hanger for the ornament by bending a 4-inch piece of wire into a loop, and twisting the ends tightly together.

Push the ends of the wire loop between the flowers into the top of the ball.

Now attach a small velvet bow to the top of the ornament with a few drops of glue.

Gilded Fruit Ornaments

MATERIALS NEEDED:

small clusters of miniature plastic fruit
flat black spray enamel
Treasure Gold Wax Gilt
velvet ribbon—¼ inch wide; 10 inches for each cluster of fruit
black heavy duty thread

DIRECTIONS:

Spray the fruit completely with black enamel.

When the enamel is dry, rub Treasure Gold on the fruit with your fingers in short, uneven strokes. Apply just a light coat of gold, and let the black show through in various places.

Tie a flattering velvet bow to the stem of each fruit cluster, and a small loop made of heavy duty thread so the ornament may be hung from your tree.

Sequined Tree Decorations

MATERIALS NEEDED:

small clusters of miniature plastic fruit
½-inch brass sequin pins
sequins—an assortment of brilliant colors to cover the fruit
velvet ribbon—¼ inch wide in a color of your choice; about 10 inches for each ornament
black heavy duty thread

DIRECTIONS:

Cover each piece of fruit with sequins by putting a pin through the center hole of each sequin and pushing the pin into the fruit.

When you have finished covering the fruit with sequins, tie a small loop of heavy duty thread to the stems so the fruit may be hung on your tree.

Then attach a velvet bow to each fruit cluster for added eye appeal.

String and Ribbon Bulbs

MATERIALS NEEDED:

small round balloons—1 for each bulb

heavy string—get a large roll if you intend to make a number of bulbs

wallpaper paste

semigloss or gloss spray enamel—any color

velvet ribbon, ¾ inch wide, about 18 inches for each string bulb

scissors

white glue

sequins—1 or several colors

black heavy duty thread

DIRECTIONS:

To make one bulb, fill a balloon with air and close the opening at the top.

Mix wallpaper paste with water until it is the consistency of very thick soup.

Then soak about 3 yards of string in the paste.

When the string is thoroughly drenched with paste, wrap and wind it around the balloon. This does not have to be done in any particular

pattern, or using any special system. Just keep crisscrossing and overlapping the string until you have a fine meshwork of string.

Leave a small area around the opening of the balloon uncovered so the balloon may be removed when the paste dries.

DON'T COVER WITH STRING

Tie a string around the neck of the balloon, and hang it up until the paste is dry. A shower curtain rod or clothesline is a suitable place to hang the balloon.

When the paste has dried and the string is hard, remove the balloon from the bulb. To do this, deflate the balloon by pricking it with a pin and pull it through the opening in the top of the bulb.

Next, paint the bulb with as many coats of spray enamel as are necessary to cover the string. Be sure to let the paint dry after each application.

When the paint has dried, glue a strip of velvet ribbon around the bulb, and attach a bow to cover the opening at the top.

Glue sequins to the ribbon or string, and tie a loop of heavy duty black thread near the top of the bulb.

Papier-mâché Balls

MATERIALS NEEDED:

styrofoam balls
wallpaper paste
flexible wire
wire cutters
newspaper
Treasure Gold Wax Gilt
semigloss enamel—any color or a variety of colors
paint brush
turpentine
string, beads, rickrack, braid or lace —to trim the balls

DIRECTIONS:

The basic directions for making all papier-mâché balls are the same, although each ornament may be trimmed and painted differently.

First, cut a 4-inch piece of wire and bend it into a loop, twisting the ends tightly together.

Push the twisted ends of the wire into the styrofoam ball so only the loop can be seen. This will make it possible to hang the ball on your Christmas tree.

Next, prepare the wallpaper paste by mixing it with water until it's fairly soupy, and tear newspaper into tiny squares, and soak in paste.

Cover the entire ball with two or three layers of paste-soaked squares, rubbing each square smoothly in place with your fingers.

To embellish the ornament, wind and glue rickrack, braid, string or lace around the ball. Beads may also be attached with glue.

Then let the ball set until the papier-mâché is perfectly dry.

Paint the ball with enamel. One solid color or several contrasting colors may be used. Let this dry, and apply another coat of paint if necessary.

When the final coat of paint has dried, rub on Treasure Gold with your fingers, using short, uneven strokes. This will give the ornament a warm, golden glow.

Papier-mâché Flower Chains

MATERIALS NEEDED:

cardboard or poster board
wallpaper paste
stapler
red and green semigloss enamel
paint brush
turpentine
red and green sequins
scissors
white glue

green or red velvet ribbon—¼ inch wide; about 15 inches long for a chain of 3 flowers
black heavy duty thread
Treasure Gold Wax Gilt (*optional*)

DIRECTIONS:

For each flower you will need to cut two layers of petals from cardboard.

One layer of petals should be made slightly smaller than the other.

To join the two layers of petals, place the smaller one on top of the larger one and staple them together.

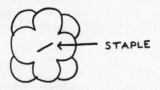

Bend the petals up a little bit to give them a perky look.

Next, mix wallpaper paste with water until it is quite thick—about the consistency of oatmeal.

Cover every portion of the flower with paste by rubbing it on with your fingers, applying it generously to the top of each petal. This will give the petals a lightly textured appearance when dry.

Follow this procedure to make as many flowers as you wish.

After this has been done, put the flowers away until the papier-mâché is perfectly dry.

Paint some of the flowers with red enamel and others with green. Let them dry, apply a second coat of paint, and dry again.

Then cover the center of each red flower with green sequins, and each green flower with red sequins glued into place.

Treasure Gold may be rubbed onto the tips of each petal to give the flowers shine and polish.

Now link two or more flowers together to form a chain. To do this, cut a 2½-inch piece of velvet ribbon, and glue one end of it to the bottom petal of the first flower. Glue the other end of the ribbon to the top petal of the second flower.

Attach additional flowers in the same manner.

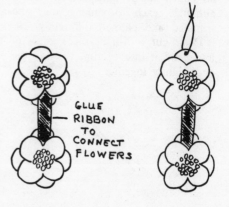

Finally, poke a tiny hole in the top petal of the first flower and insert a small loop of heavy duty thread.

Hide the hole with a velvet bow glued into place.

Candle Extravaganza

When is a candle more than a candle? When it's glorified by gold filigree and frosted with miniature snowballs. Then it's a candle extravaganza!

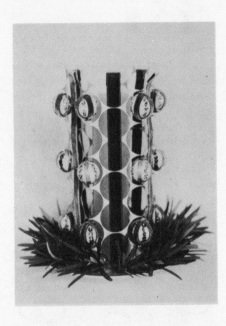

MATERIALS NEEDED:

1 air-conditioner filter—buy the type which looks like a brass screen. Unlike a regular window screen, the holes or openings in this are about 1½ inches in diameter.

12 styrofoam balls—about 1 inch in diameter

1 large candle

sequins—1 color or a number of colors

flat plate or dish—to be used as a base

½-inch brass sequin pins

velvet ribbon—¼ inch wide; 2 or 3 yards

velvet ribbon—¾ inch wide; about 2 yards long

thread—to match the color of the velvet ribbon

scissors

wire cutters

DIRECTIONS:

Using wire cutters, remove the rectangular brass screen from the air-conditioner filter.

Roll the screen into a cylinder, and bend the ends of the metal together at the back of the cylinder to keep it in this shape.

Create vertical velvet stripes on the cylinder by weaving ¾-inch ribbon in and out of the openings in the screen. Do this to ONLY every other vertical row of holes.

To hold the stripes in place, overlap and glue the ends of each piece of ribbon to the inside of the cylinder.

Next, decorate the styrofoam balls with velvet ribbon and sequins.

Begin by gluing a strip of ¼-inch velvet ribbon around the ball. Then glue another strip around the ball, crossing the first strip at right angles. This will give the ornament the appearance of being divided into four sections.

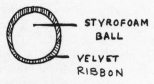

STYROFOAM BALL

VELVET RIBBON

SIDE VIEW

Add sequins to dress up the styrofoam that is still visible by placing a pin in the middle of each sequin and pushing it into the styrofoam.

Push a straight pin into the top of each ornament and tie a small piece of thread to the head of the pin. Use this to fasten the bulb to the cylinder.

Suspend the balls in any 12 of the openings of the cylinder not already filled with velvet ribbon.

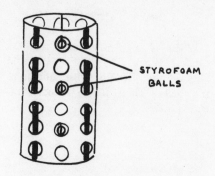

STYROFOAM BALLS

Now put the cylinder on a flat plate or dish, surround it with greenery, and place a large candle inside.

Curious Christmas Tree

This odd little tree has an unusual grace. Your guests may find

it mystifyingly familiar, but they'll never guess its origin!

1 metal spiral-shaped spring—from an old bed or chair. If you haven't one available, this may be bought in an upholstery shop.
1 block of wood—about 2 inches thick and 5 inches square
metallic gold spray paint
tiny round Christmas tree ornaments —any color
epoxy glue
small metal bottle cover—to be used to hold the candle
sandpaper—fine and very fine grades
1 tall candle

Let the glue set until hard, and spray the spring and wooden block with gold paint.

When the paint is dry, hang as many tiny ornaments as possible from the coiled wire.

Then insert a tall candle into the bottle cover by gently lowering the candle down through the middle of the tree.

DIRECTIONS:

Sand the block of wood with fine and then very fine sandpaper until it's perfectly smooth. Be sure to wipe off all dust when you're through sanding.

Use epoxy glue to attach an upside-down bottle cover to the top of the wood, centering it carefully.

Sleigh Centerpiece

Spring and winter merge to make this charming centerpiece of wild ripe strawberries nestled deep among sprigs of dark green holly.

Next, glue the larger end of the spring to the top of the wooden block.

Holding the stems, dip the berries and the holly into this mixture.

Use clothespins to hang each strawberry and cluster of holly upside down on a clothesline to dry. Shake the line occasionally so any excess paint will fall off.

When the sleigh, berries and holly are dry, put the arrangement together.

Heap the berries into the sleigh, letting them spill out over the sides.

Cut the holly into small sprigs, and push them in between the berries.

MATERIALS NEEDED:

straw or reed sleigh
spray enamel—flat, semigloss or gloss. Choose black, red, green or white.
plastic strawberries—enough to fill the sleigh abundantly. Any red berry may be used, such as cherries or raspberries.
small plastic holly leaves and berries
½ pint light oak varnish
½ pint gloss varnish
½ pint turpentine
empty coffee can
straight pin
clothespins
⅔ yard red or green velvet ribbon —1 inch wide

Add a bow of brilliant red or green velvet and attach it to the front of the sleigh with a straight pin.

Tree Skirt

If your Christmas budget seems to be soaring out of sight (as it generally does), you've probably felt you couldn't afford one of these gala tree skirts.

You can make your own for about half the price of those you've seen on display in various boutique shops and have the fun of selecting your own design.

Whether you choose to sprinkle it with glittering stars, colorful toy

DIRECTIONS:

Spray the sleigh with the enamel you have selected. Apply as many coats as necessary to cover the straw or reed completely, letting the paint dry after each application.

Mix the ½ pint light oak varnish, the ½ pint turpentine and the ½ pint gloss varnish in an empty coffee can.

soldiers, miniature trees, flirtatious snowmen or the conventional partridge, it's guaranteed to dress your tree in high fashion.

MATERIALS NEEDED:

1 square yard felt—red, green or any color of your choice
scissors
pencil
4 yards ball fringe—a color to match or complement the felt
thread
needle or sewing machine
white glue
felt—10-inch squares in a variety of colors appropriate to the decorations you intend to add to the tree skirt
trimmings (*optional*)—yarn, sequins, beads, lace, rickrack or fancy braid

DIRECTIONS:

It takes very little effort to construct the basic tree skirt, because felt is easy to work with and needs no hemming.

Form a large circle from the square yard of felt. This can be done easily by rounding off all four corners of the square. Use a pencil to draw guide lines, and cut carefully along the lines.

ROUND OFF CORNERS

On one side of the circle make a cut from the outer edge to the center of the circle.

Then cut out a small circle, 4 inches in diameter, from the middle of the felt circle.

Finish the edges by sewing ball fringe to the circumference of the tree skirt. This may be done by hand or with a sewing machine

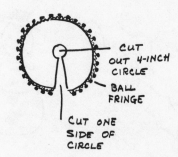

CUT OUT 4-INCH CIRCLE

BALL FRINGE

CUT ONE SIDE OF CIRCLE

There are an infinite number of ways to trim this basic tree skirt. You can keep it very simple or make it extremely ornate.

First, decide what type of decorations you want to use on the skirt. Snowmen, holly, angels, Santa Claus, partridges, toy soldiers, Christmas trees, candles, stars, candy canes and

Christmas stockings are a few ideas to choose from. You might use one subject or combine several.

Draw and cut your pattern from a piece of paper. A child's Christmas coloring book can be very helpful if you have trouble drawing your own pattern. The pictures are generally very simple and can be cut apart to be used as a pattern.

Make appliqués from felt by tracing around your pattern and cutting out the objects.

Arrange the appliqués on the tree skirt in an interesting manner and glue them in place.

Use felt of contrasting colors to add details to the appliqués, attaching it with glue.

If you wish to make the appliqués more elaborate, use glue or thread to attach sequins, lace, beads, yarn designs or fancy braid.

Here are a few patterns you might enlarge and try

Papier-mâché Bells

There's a different sound and a special sweetness to the chimes, as they sing out the joyful message of Christmas night.

These golden bells will grace your home and put the song of Christmas in your heart.

MATERIALS NEEDED:

2 bells—styrofoam or plastic
newspaper
wallpaper paste
flexible wire
wire cutters
1½ yards lace—about ½ inch wide
gloss or semigloss enamel—red, green
  or a color of your choice. Use
  spray or regular brushing enamel.
Treasure Gold Wax Gilt

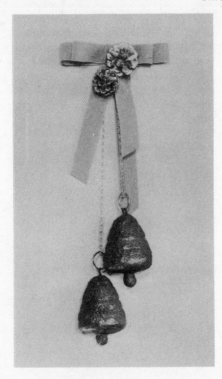

Push the twisted ends of the wire into the top of the styrofoam or plastic bell so only the loop can be seen. Make one loop for each bell in this manner.

Mix the wallpaper paste with water until it's about the consistency of oatmeal, and tear newspaper into tiny squares, and soak in paste.

Cover both bells completely with two or three layers of paste-soaked squares, rubbing each square smoothly in place with your fingers.

Add two or three rows of lace to the sides of each bell. Soak the lace in the wallpaper paste and affix it to the bell.

24 inches brass chain—fairly fine link chain
1½ yards velvet ribbon—2 inches wide; in a color to complement the paint
pliers
scissors
2 brass rings—each should be about 1 inch in diameter
paint brush
turpentine
2 or 3 pine cones
pine boughs (*optional*)

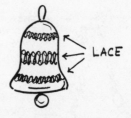

Let the bells set until the papier-mâché is bone dry.

Paint the bells with two coats of enamel, letting them dry thoroughly after each application.

DIRECTIONS:

Begin by cutting a 4-inch piece of wire. Bend it into a loop and twist the ends tightly together.

Then give the bells a golden sheen by rubbing on Treasure Gold with your fingers, using short, uneven strokes. Be sure to let some of the underlying color show through the gold.

Mix a little turpentine with Treasure Gold. Using a brush, paint the pine cones with this mixture. You don't have to paint the whole pine cone. Just brush the gold onto the tips of the petals to make them glisten.

Use pliers to open the brass rings a little bit, and connect one ring to each end of the chain.

Slip the wire loops on top of the bells onto the brass rings, one on each end of the chain.

Close the rings again with the pliers.

Wire the back of the pine cones together, and attach these to one link in the middle of the brass chain.

Tie a large bow from the velvet ribbon. Then fasten the pine cones and chain to the center knot of the bow with a small piece of wire.

If you wish, several pine boughs may be wired to the back of the velvet bow as a background for the bells.

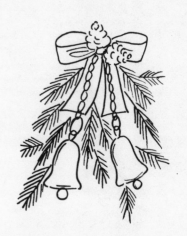

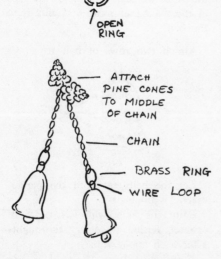

OPEN RING

ATTACH PINE CONES TO MIDDLE OF CHAIN

CHAIN

BRASS RING

WIRE LOOP

Fabric Christmas Tree

Christmas trees have a way of giving a lift to your heart, your spirits and your smile, so the more the merrier!

No matter how many trees you have, you're sure to find room for this elegant little tree of deep green velvet and molten gold.

MATERIALS NEEDED:

styrofoam cone—10 inches high
small can, bottle or spray can cover
　—to be used as the base of the
　tree. It should be a little smaller
　in diameter than the bottom of the
　styrofoam cone.

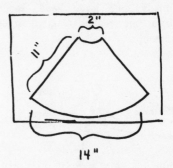

Spread glue evenly on the back of the fabric and attach it to the cone.

Measure and cut a piece of velvet to cover the sides of the can, bottle or spray can cover and attach it with glue.

Then glue the fabric-covered can or bottle to the bottom of the styrofoam cone to make a base for the tree.

CAN OR BOTTLE

15 square inches green velvet—or any green fabric
2 yards gold braid—1 yard of two different styles
straight pins
white glue
24 inches green ball fringe
sequins or beads—beads from an inexpensive necklace are good
scissors
ruler

DIRECTIONS:

Cover the styrofoam cone with green velvet, using the pattern provided for cutting the velvet.

Wrap the velvet around the cone to see how it fits. If it's too long or too wide, use scissors to trim it to the proper size.

Attach two rows of ball fringe to the tree, one at the bottom to hide the raw edges of the velvet, and the other in the middle of the tree. Use glue or straight pins to fasten the fringe to the tree.

Then add seven or eight rows of gold braid to the tree with glue or straight pins. Place one row of braid around the very top of the cone to cover the edge of the fabric.

Decorate the tree, between the rows of ball fringe and braid, with sequins or beads. Use a straight pin, pushed through the hole in each sequin or bead, to attach them to the tree.

Finally, one large bead, secured with a pin, makes a good treetop ornament.

metal statues. Their quiet warmth will fill your home—and your heart —with the joyous spirit of the Christmas season.

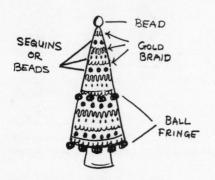

Gilded Manger Scene

An atmosphere of serene beauty surrounds this glowing replica of the first Christmas. The figurines are made to resemble authentic cast-

MATERIALS NEEDED:

inexpensive plaster figurines
fast-drying flat black spray enamel
Treasure Gold Wax Gilt

DIRECTIONS:

Spray the figures with enough coats of enamel to cover the original finish.

When this has dried, rub on Treasure Gold with your fingers. Do not cover deep folds or detail lines with gold, but let the black show through. This will give the figurines an antiquated, tarnished appearance.

Polish with a soft, clean cloth until the gold becomes lustrous.

ALL-SEASON TREE

Have you yearned to change the sometimes monotonous order of things? Give vent to those too-often-suppressed rebellious instincts and urges with this versatile "tree." Whether it's a realistic blossoming bough or a fantasy of sugarplums, lollipops and gingerbread men, it's a tree of a thousand marvels and infinite interest because you make it whatever you please!

MATERIALS NEEDED:

1 dried tree branch, without the leaves
flowerpot
green styrofoam—to fit inside the pot
flat or semigloss spray enamel—any color. (The tree may be painted a different color each time the decorations are changed.)

DIRECTIONS:

To make the basic tree, spray the entire branch with enamel; be sure to cover it completely with paint.

When the paint is dry, push the trunk of your tree firmly into the styrofoam which has been placed inside the flowerpot.

Now the fun begins!

Any small, lightweight object can be attached to the tree with thread, tape, wire or string. With a smattering of ingenuity and materials, you can furnish this tree with an unusual attire for every occasion, season or party.

Remember, ANYTHING can grow on your tree, no matter how outlandish Mother Nature would find it!

Here are several hints to get you started

If, for example, you're snowed in under ten feet of snow and the blizzard shows no signs of letting up, distract your attention from the freeze with a flowering cherry tree. Or if you're sweltering in the summer heat, make any room a cool oasis of rain-sweet leaves and crisply scented pine cones.

Bring the salty tang of the sea into your home with a sea-shell tree, or hang your tree with fishing flies, bobbers and colorful lures.

In an exuberant and childlike mood, you might create a sugarplum tree of gumdrops, jelly beans, licorice sticks and candy canes—the kind you used to dream about!

At Christmastime the tree can sprout green and red velvet bows and miniature ornaments or become the traditional pear tree for a partridge, by displaying plastic pears and flaunting an artificial bird.

Special holidays offer a good excuse for changing the foliage of your tree. Let it bloom with Easter eggs, valentines, pumpkins and black cats, or with St. Patrick's favorite flower, the shamrock.

Fabricate a friendship tree by hanging photographs of your friends and relatives from the branches. Each picture may be framed by cutting the picture and gluing it to the inside of a small bottle cover which has been painted gold.

And in answer to that all-too-frequent (and generally masculine) remark that "money doesn't grow on trees," make yourself a money tree, and prove that money CAN grow on trees!

Or simply make a tree which blooms and bears antiqued flowers and fruits all year long.

This is literally a tree for all seasons!

Shopping Sources for Supplies and Equipment

air-conditioner filter
hardware store

American flag (small)
dime store

ball fringe
dime store or fabric shop

balloons
dime store

beads (inexpensive necklace)
dime store

braid (silver, gold, etc., for trimming)
dime store or yard goods store

brass chain
hardware store

brass rings
hardware store

burlap
yard goods store

cake plate (inexpensive, plastic)
dime store

candleholders (glass)
dime store

candles
dime store

chain
hardware store

chicken wire
lumberyard or hardware store

child's modeling clay
dime store

colander (metal)
dime store

crepe paper
dime store

doilies
dime store

doweling
hardware store or lumberyard

drawing paper
dime store or art supply store

drinking straws (paper or plastic)
supermarket or dime store

enamel (hobby, in ¼ oz. bottles)
dime store or hobby shop

felt
dime store or yard goods store

figurines (plaster)
dime store

florist clay
dime store or florist shop

florist tape
dime store or florist shop

flowerpot (clay)
dime store

fringe or braid
dime store or yard goods store

glasses (parfait or wine)
dime store

gold paint
dime store or hardware store

individual metal molds for gelatin desserts and salads
  dime store

lace
  dime store or yard goods store

net
  dime store or yard goods store

nut cups (paper or cardboard)
  dime store

nuts (in the shell)
  grocery store or supermarket

paint
  hardware, dime or paint store

picture hangers
  dime store or hardware store

pine cones (real or artificial)
  florist shop or piney woods

pipe cleaners
  dime store or drug store

plastic flowers
  dime store

plastic fruit
  dime store

plastic leaves
  dime store

poster board (white or colored)
  dime store or art supply store

ribbon
  dime store

rickrack or braid
  dime store or yard goods store

sequin pins
  dime store or hobby shop

sequins
  dime store or hobby shop

sleigh (reed or straw)
  dime store

straw basket
  dime store

styrofoam (balls, cones, rings, bells, etc.)
  dime store or hobby shop

tin cutters (inexpensive)
  dime store or hardware store

tissue paper
  dime store or art supply store

toy drum and drumsticks
  dime store

Treasure Gold Wax Gilt
  hobby shop, hardware or art supply store

varnish (gloss or semigloss)
  dime store, hardware or paint store

wallpaper paste
  paint or hardware store

watering can (metal or plastic)
  hardware or dime store

white drawing paper
  dime store or art supply store

wire
  hardware store or dime store

yarn
  dime store